DESTINATION; REMARKABLE.

DESTINATION: REMARKABLE.

SURVIVING

THE DARK SIDE

OF SUCCESS

MARY GROTHE

Forbes | Books

Published by Forbes Books, Charleston, South Carolina.
An imprint of Advantage Media Group.

Forbes Books is a registered trademark, and the Forbes Books colophon is a trademark of Forbes Media, LLC.

Printed in the United States of America.

10 9 8 7 6 5 4 3 2 1

ISBN: 979-8-88750-054-6 (Hardcover)
ISBN: 979-8-88750-055-3 (eBook)

Library of Congress Control Number: 2023906395

Book design by Analisa Smith.

This custom publication is intended to provide accurate information and the opinions of the author in regard to the subject matter covered. It is sold with the understanding that the publisher, Forbes Books, is not engaged in rendering legal, financial, or professional services of any kind. If legal advice or other expert assistance is required, the reader is advised to seek the services of a competent professional.

Since 1917, Forbes has remained steadfast in its mission to serve as the defining voice of entrepreneurial capitalism. Forbes Books, launched in 2016 through a partnership with Advantage Media, furthers that aim by helping business and thought leaders bring their stories, passion, and knowledge to the forefront in custom books. Opinions expressed by Forbes Books authors are their own. To be considered for publication, please visit **books.Forbes.com**.

*To my husband and son ... thank you for
loving me just as I am and allowing me to
be an imperfect and fearless risk-taker.*

BOARDING PASS

ECONOMY

PASSENGER
Mary Grothe

DEPARTURE
9:39am
Valparaiso, IN
ORD

ARRIVAL
11:27am
Denver, CO
DIA

Flight CA3823
Terminal B

GATE
12

BOARDING
9:09AM

SEAT
14A

PASSENGER
Mary Grothe

Flight CA3823
Terminal B

GATE
12

BOARDING
9:09AM

SEAT
14A

CLOUD★AIR

CONTENTS

FOREWORD

FOREWORD

estination; Remarkable: The Dark Side of Success is a provocative narrative of Mary's courageous and challenging life. Without withholding, she shares the real and the raw that most are unwilling to share. This is rare. So many hide the experiences that have made them, often out of shame or embarrassment. Mary does not. She dives deeply into her journey and her healing, into what made her who she is today.

Most want to hide and ignore their dark shadows–many of us spend a lot of time denying, deflecting, or dismissing them. Shame, guilt, anger, and resentment are not popular themes, for example, on social media. But our shadows make us who we are, and by disowning them, we disown an important piece of ourselves. Mary's courage, intention, and willingness to explore and share the dark side of her success will inspire you to do the same in your life. Her faith and trust are palpable–you will feel it on each page. The more you read, the more you'll recognize that you're not alone.

The Mary Grothe I met years ago was in hiding. During our initial meeting, she danced around my questions, and generally seemed aloof and slippery. She seemed like a little girl who was afraid, yet skilled at leveraging her intellect to manipulate and control. Yet I still had a sense of what was happening beneath the surface: between her beautiful heart and the image she wanted to project to others was a layer of armor.

Years of shadowboxing–protecting her heart with that image and that armor–were clearly, subtly taking a toll. Eventually, that armor cracked, and I became a witness to the transformation you too will witness throughout the book. She began to see that it's possible to live life without that armor, without hiding her true self.

This book is a liberation–not only for Mary, but for women and men who are protecting themselves from their shadows, who want to be free, but who don't know how to take the first step. There are so many themes that Mary unabashedly explores here: self-worth, validation, pleasing others to be loved and acknowledged, shame, guilt, the pull of the material world…and in the end, the recognition that the only way out of this spiral is through the inward journey.

Mary's inward journey ultimately centers on her faith and her love for Christ. Going inward and trusting in God's path is challenging, but rewarding. Mary's newfound peace, contentment, and fulfillment in her personal *and* professional life is the result of this courageous journey, as well as her willingness to trust, surrender, and co-create with God.

Mary has set the stage here for you to step across a threshold–one that perhaps you too may have also been avoiding. Reading this book will challenge you–not only to heal and transcend the stories and wounds of your past, but to create a foundation for the future, both for yourself, and for humanity. You'll see: liberation and freedom are on the other side for you, too.

–Doug McGhee
CEO, Realm.men

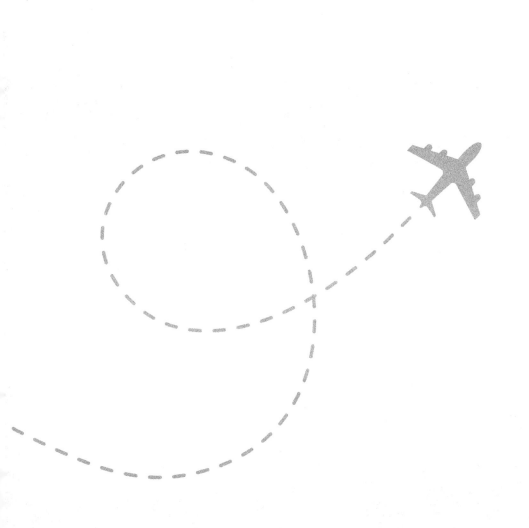

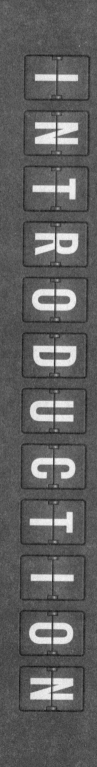

INTRODUCTION

This is the very first time I've ever shared my story in its entirety. Some parts of it are out in the world here and there, but I've always left out several details, partly because I didn't want to be judged. I also didn't particularly want to remember or relive it.

Now that I have, I want to state up front that I've completely forgiven everyone in my family and beyond. I deeply believe that nobody maliciously set out to hurt me. We're all flawed human beings. We're all sinners, and we all make mistakes—I've made plenty, and we'll get into that too. I've hurt a lot of people myself, but I never had malicious intent. Like any of us, I was doing the best I could with what I had at that moment.

This story comes from a place of grace, mercy, and forgiveness, and I have no ill will toward anyone. I'm sharing it so that I can help other people who might be facing similar situations. My hope is that they'll be able to read or listen to this and say, *She overcame the exact same thing that I'm dealing with. What an inspiration.* I'm going to be as raw and vulnerable as I can.

With that said, let's spill some tea.

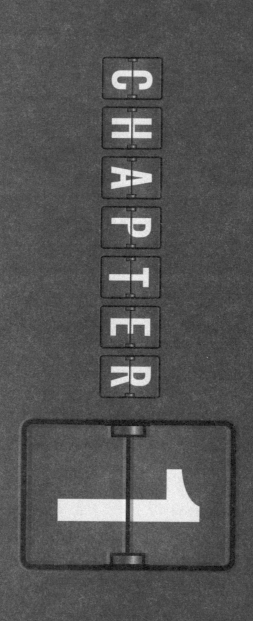

CHAPTER 1

I grew up in a big, beautiful, creepy Victorian house in Valparaiso, Indiana. Being a little girl in a big house, I probably felt it was bigger than it really was. It had no basement, but there was a cold, damp cellar with a dirt floor, and we'd go down there when bad weather or tornadoes came through. I still have recurring nightmares about it.

Most of all, I remember what we called the *green room*, where we kept our piano. My mom was a classical pianist, and she would play for hours and hours. She was so talented, and I loved listening to her. My dad was an opera singer and an actor—also unbelievably talented. He sounded just like Pavarotti—you could listen to the two of them back to back and not tell the difference.

My parents were also born in northwest Indiana. Both my mom's parents were alcoholics, and her upbringing was terrible. Dysfunction and abuse were par for the course. My dad grew up in a second-generation Greek family, and his first marriage was to his high school sweetheart. If I remember right, after they got divorced, she went off and married his best friend.

My parents met after my dad's divorce—to this day, I still don't know how or where—and my mom brought along two daughters from her previous marriage. My mom had her first daughter when she was eighteen, which led to her getting married, as that's just what you did back then. My brother was born in 1982, and then I came along a year and a half later, in November of 1983.

One of my earliest memories is being two years old, wearing my red-footed pajamas, and hearing my mom and then-eighteen-year-old sister having a brutal fight, screaming at one another. After that, my sister moved out, and I didn't see her again for years. My other sister was the one who mostly took care of us—she was more of a mom to us than my mom was, and for that she incurred my mom's wrath.

My parents were smokers, so there were ashtrays everywhere. The wallpaper was stained from all the smoke, and the formerly white lace curtains had turned yellowish orange. My mom had allergies, so she was always blowing her nose, wadding up the used tissue, and setting it on whatever was close at hand. If there was nothing close at hand, she'd just toss it on the floor. Because she blew her nose dozens of times a day, the used tissues accumulated everywhere, like snowdrifts.

I grew up in absolute filth. We had a dog and four cats, and they had accidents all over the house. That house was disgustingly dirty from top to bottom, but I was used to it and didn't really know any better until I was a teenager. The bank ultimately seized the house, tore it down, and turned it into a parking lot, and I'm happy they did. That house was full of demons, and I still think of it as a dark and scary place.

When I was three, my parents opened a performing arts school. There was a little store attached to it where we'd sell sheet music, accessories, instruments, ballet shoes, and tights—whatever our students needed. My fifteen-year-old sister did a lot of the administrative work, and the rest of us were always printing and stapling brochures.

I was the first student enrolled in the dance program, and when I took my first ballet class, I fell in love. I remember how nervous I was to start—I wasn't going to go through with it unless my brother did it with me, so he got enrolled too. Soon, we were all roped into acting, singing, and dance, and I also started studying piano. As early as three or four, I was in everything from *Cat on a Hot Tin Roof* to *Annie* to *Willy Wonka & the Chocolate Factory* to *The Nut-*

> **I was the first student enrolled in the dance program, and when I took my first ballet class, I fell in love.**

cracker. My dad played Tevye in *Fiddler on the Roof*, and I was little Chava.

I absolutely loved being on stage. My dad gave me singing lessons, and I was singing opera by age nine. When he started touring as an opera singer, I became part of his performance troupe, and we traveled all over. I was the page turner for my mom when she accompanied him on piano. There was always something, whether annual recitals or multiperformance Christmas choirs. In downtown Valparaiso, there was a community theater guild that put on multiple shows per year, and we were always in them as a family. The mayor and his wife were my godparents, and my dad and I even performed at their inaugural luncheon ball.

My entire life was dancing, singing, performing, and acting. Orville Redenbacher is from our part of Indiana, and Valparaiso has an annual popcorn festival and parade in his name. We'd always bake hundreds of batches of popcorn, string it through with thread, and hang it on a float advertising our performing arts school. We frequently drove an hour west to Chicago, stayed at the ornate Palmer House hotel, listened to all the bands playing in the Grant Park band shell downtown, went to the symphony, and got to see *Les Misérables, Miss*

Saigon, and all the other Broadway shows. My dad used to perform at the famous Second City improv school and was cast in movies whenever they filmed in Chicago.

While all these wonderful things were going on, my mom was a raging alcoholic. She drank every single day. She'd start with coffee and cream in the morning, then would gradually switch over to White Russians in the same mug. As they day wore on, she'd become increasingly drunk, mean, and awful. Then, when she ran out of liquor, she'd throw us and even our friends into the back of the station wagon and drive drunk to the liquor store for more.

Meanwhile, my dad always struggled with what we'll call *sexual indecency.* From high school on, he always had these demons and was caught several times doing things he shouldn't be doing—I'll just leave it at that. I don't think anything ever happened to me—at least I don't have any memories of it, and for that I'm extremely grateful. Meanwhile, my mom knew about it, and she and my dad put him through treatment, but he was never formally charged with anything. Partly as a result of all this, my dad was in a constant state of depression.

Needless to say, this made for a very unhealthy marriage. No one could ever stand up to my mom, including my dad. The amount of cursing and screaming that came out of her is hard to believe in retrospect. I'm grateful that it wasn't a habit of hers to beat us, but she was certainly verbally, emotionally, and mentally abusive.

One of the main problems with alcoholic parents is never knowing when you're in trouble or what you were doing right, because the rules change every day. We wanted to behave and do the right thing, but one day you're told to do one thing, then get in trouble for doing that same thing the next. The rules would completely reverse at a moment's notice.

My mom was also a pathological liar, and her stories would always change. She had a filter on her perception: everybody was out to get her, she was always the victim, and her life was terrible. Woe is me. Doom and gloom. A scarcity mindset pervaded: we never had enough, and we were always poor. Being raised that way formed a lot of my unconscious belief systems. I was trained to think that I never had enough and that I never *was* enough. I was always in trouble, I never did anything right, and no matter what I did, it was never good enough.

Being raised in such a hellish environment, I was always seeking any glimmer of love or recognition I could find, and the only consistent way to get anything resembling love from my mom was to bring home good grades. One of the rare times she would acknowledge or praise me was when I brought home my report card. She would say, "It's your dad's and my responsibility to go to work and provide for our family. That's *our* job. *You* also have one job, and that's to go to school to get straight As." That was the one thing that was in my control, so from kindergarten through high school, I got straight As. It was nonnegotiable.

The other way I sought approval was through performing. Whenever I did well on stage or at rehearsal, sang on key, or played the right notes, and especially when I performed when I didn't want to, I could usually get some kudos.

Every day I would go to regular school, do my homework between classes, then head straight to our performing arts school, where I'd be in class or rehearsal until late at night. At least six days a week, there were always classes, rehearsals, and performances. I remember occasionally putting up a stink because I was so tired, but whenever I managed to keep my mouth shut and do exactly what my mom wanted, I could usually get some praise and recognition. This turned into what I'd call performance-based love, which would come back later to haunt me.

My brother and I were very close in age, and we fought hard and deeply hated each other. We had the worst sibling rivalry I've ever seen. I'd throw his toys in the garbage right before the garbage truck arrived. He'd spend hours building towers out of building blocks; then I'd smash right through them. In retaliation, he would take my cat and swing her around by her tail, throw her across the room, or push her off two-story ledges. One time, when he snuck up and cut my hair, I threw the scissors at his face, and they only narrowly missed his eye.

I'm sure the difficulty of raising us contributed to my mom's downward spiral, and I imagine a lot of her anger came from the fact that we never got along. But we didn't have a lot of love and compassion modeled for us—it was mostly yelling and screaming. In the end, my brother and I learned how to manage our feelings from our parents. It's a terrible cycle.

In the end, my brother and I learned how to manage our feelings from our parents. It's a terrible cycle.

Deep down, I believe my mom loved me. And I know, at the very least, that she was proud of me for doing so well in the arts and getting good grades. She always used to say, "I had to have four children until I had one that _____," and she'd fill in the blank with something like "followed in her mom's footsteps" or "plays piano" or "always gets straight As" or even "cooked full family dinners at age seven." She would never directly tell me that she loved me, but I would hear her tell other people nice things. She'd brag about me to others, then continue being nasty and awful to me behind the scenes.

It was confusing to never get that love, support, or recognition from her one on one. I think she was so broken on the inside that she needed to brag to other people, hear the words coming out of her own mouth, and then maybe try to believe them a little bit. But in the end, her demons and her disease were more in control. Unfortunately, showing someone that you love them is not a priority for those diseases—of course, it's quite the opposite.

As our family's performing arts school failed to make any money, my parents converted it into a nonprofit. They thought being tax exempt might help spur things along, but unfortunately, things just continued to go downhill. Because the business wasn't profitable, they started to forgo paychecks, then had to take out a second mortgage on our house to scrounge together some money. When that was exhausted, they had to start searching for part-time jobs and ended up taking a gig delivering newspapers.

They didn't want to leave us home alone, so they'd wake us up in the middle of the night to pile us into the back of our station wagon, where we'd try to continue sleeping in the back seat until returning around dawn. They'd chain-smoke the entire time, and I still get nauseated thinking of the smell of the smoke mingling with that of the newspapers. Winters in northern Indiana are brutal, so they'd have the windows rolled up, and the smoke was so dense you couldn't even breathe. I had to put my head inside of my coat or underneath a blanket to try to avoid breathing it all in. My brother and I eventually had to pitch in and became part of a rolling assembly line: cutting the ties for the bags, rolling, rubber-banding, and then bagging the papers.

I don't remember specifically how long my parents had that newspaper route, but it wasn't sustainable. Their next hustle was doing several affiliate fundraisers, selling cookie dough, chocolates, or gifts from Christmas catalogs, sometimes all at the same time. As soon as they made some money from those, they started neglecting to pay back all the fundraising companies, and their debts to them climbed into the thousands of dollars.

Despite all this, I only figured out that we were in real financial trouble when people in the community started delivering groceries to us. One day someone knocked on our back screen door, and by the time I got there to answer it, there was a car driving off and a few bags of food left on the stoop.

Then, one summer day when I was fourteen, my parents finally came clean. "For the last year or two, we've been trying to pay the bills and keep the school alive, and we just can't keep up with it anymore. We're behind on our mortgage payments. The bank is taking the house. We're getting foreclosed on, and we are resigning from the school, leaving the fate in the board's hands."

Then they informed us that we would also immediately be moving to Boulder, Colorado. A few hours later, an auction company arrived and pitched a giant red-and-white tent in our backyard. Then, piece by piece, they started moving everything out of our house and onto folding tables under the tent, numbered the items, and started preparing for a live auction in our backyard. Soon, people showed up and bought our belongings. It was so surreal.

I hadn't seen my oldest sister in a very long time, and meanwhile, my other sister had gotten married and moved out of the house. After that memorable feud, my oldest sister and my mom had not been on speaking terms. Soon after that big top went up in our backyard, my oldest sister showed up—with a baby. It was crazy to see her after all those years, and none of us had any idea she had a child.

I was full of fear because I knew how much hatred there was between my sister and my mom. I think they had some kind of verbal altercation that day, but it didn't happen directly in front of me. I remember being scared to death that my mom might even *see* me talking to my sister. I felt so torn—I wanted so badly to see her, hug her, and talk to her, but I also didn't want to get yelled at or deal with any fallout with my mom.

At the same time, in a sick way, I knew my mom was hurting through this whole experience, and as her child, I felt responsible for comforting her and making sure that she was okay. I could see how hard it was on my parents to lose our house and all our belongings, and my sister's appearance was the icing on the cake.

I had two days to say goodbye to my friends, our extended family, and everything else that I knew. I was fourteen, had just finished eighth grade, and thought I was about to be going into high school with all my friends. I still had a full slate of rehearsals and performances lined up. Then the rug got pulled out from under us. The next day, we packed the few things we had left into a moving van and drove to Colorado.

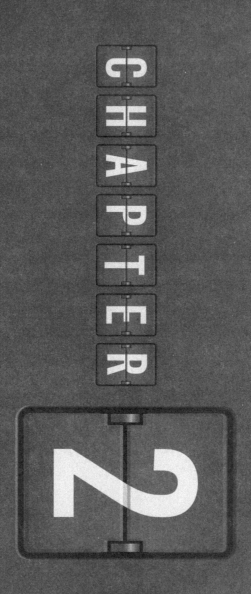

CHAPTER 2

When we got to Colorado, we stayed for a night in a hotel while waiting for our apartment to open up, and when it did, we moved right in. Right away, a cascade of new realities hit me: I knew no one here and would have to start over completely, and my parents were officially poor. After filing for bankruptcy, my dad got a job at Sears, and my mom became a receptionist at a law firm. Next, they told my brother and me that we needed to find jobs because they couldn't support our family on their dual minimum wages.

My brother started work right away, but I wasn't allowed to because I was still only fourteen. It wasn't long before my birthday rolled around in November, and I joined him bagging groceries at King Soopers. I was now responsible for paying my portion of the rent, part of our car payment, and my groceries. Like everyone else in our family, I was only making $6.60 an hour. OSHA laws prevented me from working for more than twenty hours a week, so I was barely making enough to pay what my parents demanded back home. I still wasn't old enough to have my own bank account, so my mom cosigned for me, which allowed her to take money out of my account.

Before long, I was stealing food on my breaks. I'd go past the bakery, grab a donut, and sneak upstairs to eat it. When I was bagging groceries, I'd knock things off the counter, kick them under the bagging station, then put them in my sock when no one was looking. All the baggers wore aprons with big pockets, so when it was quiet and there were no groceries to bag, I would take more food and hide it in those pockets.

Despite everything, I still wanted to continue my dance classes. I signed on with the Boulder Ballet, and not far from there was a dance studio called Dance West. One day, rather than going to ballet as usual, I got off the bus and snuck into a hip-hop class, and it changed my life. I'd never listened to that kind of music, and I absolutely fell in love—from then on, I was sneaking into whatever jazz, hip-hop, or break-dancing classes I could simply by pretending I'd already paid the monthly membership fee. In no time, I became quite the little hip-hopper and break-dancer.

At the same time, I started my freshman year at Fairview High School in Boulder. I'd been pretty far ahead academically in Indiana, where the curriculum was a little bit more advanced than it was in Colorado. In terms of making grades, my freshman year was an absolute breeze. I overloaded my classes from day one, so by the time I was a senior, I was only at school for three hours per day.

Outside of academics, my freshman year was not easy. I'd come from northwest Indiana looking like a white-bread midwestern girl: no makeup, baggy jeans, baggy shirts. I had no sense of fashion or style. None of that was important in northwest Indiana—Valparaiso was just a small postindustrial town, surrounded by cornfields. There was certainly no fashion scene to speak of.

Then, when I was thrown into my new high school in Boulder, holy smokes—I went through a fair amount of culture shock that first year, and initially, I was bullied heavily. I was a straight-A student and a total nerd, always buried in books. I didn't style my hair and was wearing big purple glasses that would be more suited to a little girl. My new fourteen-year-old classmates were a lot to take in: makeup, hair, midriffs, skintight clothes. Moreover, there are a lot of very wealthy people in Boulder. I had classmates pulling up to school in BMWs, Lexus, and Mercedes. My family was still driving our decrepit Ford Contour, which I took to King Soopers after school to bag rich people's groceries.

As a freshman, you must share a locker with someone, and my "locker buddy" was one of the popular girls—blond, beautiful,

I felt like I had to fit in and realized that if I wanted to avoid getting picked on and made fun of, I had to make some changes.

wealthy, with a boyfriend to match. I was ridiculed and made fun of by her and her friends every day—as soon as I walked up, they'd stop talking and either stare at me or burst out laughing. I didn't fit in with that group, nor did I even understand it—I had no experience with adolescent cliques from middle school in Indiana. I'd never been around anything like that, period. I was constantly embarrassed, made fun of, and talked down to, all on top of what I was dealing with back at home.

I had long naturally curly hair, and before we moved, I'd always let it air-dry. Outside of performances, I'd never styled my hair. Suddenly, I felt like I had to fit in and realized that if I wanted to avoid getting picked on and made fun of, I had to make some changes. I managed to get contact lenses and cut my hair and used my dad's employee discount at Sears to get some new clothes, but the little bit of money I had didn't go very far.

A few weeks before the start of my sophomore year, I knew I'd need a new wardrobe for school but didn't have nearly enough money. I remember taking the bus back down to the Sears where my dad worked, and my new friend Amanda and I went in with our backpacks and stole hundreds of dollars' worth of clothes.

Our little complex of townhomes had a pool, which is where Amanda and I met. She was a promiscuous, homeschooled trouble-maker and opened my eyes to the naughtier side of being a teenage girl. She became my mentor in all things fashion and makeup—she was beautiful, and of course I wanted to be beautiful too.

When our first school dance rolled around, I thought it would finally be my time to shine—*wow, look at her, she's such a good dancer*. I wasn't prepared for it to be a bunch of young teenagers dressing up in provocative clothing and bumping and grinding all over one other. When I showed up, I had no idea what to do.

When I got back home and told Amanda what happened, she knew just what to do: she immediately took out her boom box and proceeded to teach me how to move my hips to Shakira, Britney Spears, Christina Aguilera, and NSYNC. That was just the beginning of my apprenticeship, which gradually came to include taping entire episodes of Carson Daly's *Total Request Live*, studying the dance moves, and rewinding the VHS over and over until we had everything down.

This all coincided with my burgeoning love for hip-hop dance, and eventually, by the beginning of my sophomore year, I tried out for the pom squad and made the team. That helped my social cause tremendously—it gave me a new, instant friend group, which acceler-ated my transformation. By that time, I was going to school in one outfit to fool my mom, then changing into another in the bathroom as soon as I got to school.

Everything started to change. By the time I turned sixteen, I was allowed to work forty hours a week. I started making twice as much money and was able to get my mom, and her habit, out of my bank account. This all made me bolder, and I grew less timid about wearing what I wanted to wear around the house. This led to my mom calling me things like *easy* and *a slut*, which are such nice things to hear from your mom.

I had made a couple of nerdy friends my freshman year—their names were Colleen, Janine, and Kristen. They were similar to me, late-blooming book nerds—such sweet, wonderful girls, who never conformed to the pressures of high school, like I ultimately did. I'm sure each has gone on to do amazing things in life. By the time I joined the pom squad, I was on an entirely different path, and we all drifted apart.

When the time came, my dad started to teach me how to drive. I went to driver's ed, got a license, and decided to effectively buy our family car by taking over the payments. My brother didn't have any interest in driving, and I was juggling the pom squad, working, and dance classes downtown, so I really needed to drive. My mom had been walking to work since we'd moved, but my dad still needed a car, so he finally bought his own.

At that point, I basically started fully supporting myself. I still paid partial rent to live in my parents' house and increasingly did everything I could to become financially independent. I started saving my money and got a credit card—the same one I use today.

Around this time, my brother was going down a dark path. He became a goth, started cutting himself, and began to romanticize death and suicide. He was playing Dungeons & Dragons around the clock, dressing in all black, and growing his hair out, and he wasn't regularly bathing or brushing his teeth, to the extent that his teeth were orange and gray. His bedroom was like a dungeon, and he never cleaned it—every plate and bowl in the house seemed to accumulate there, and since he never washed them, there was always moldy food sitting around. The smell was horrible—he'd crack open the door to his room and you'd almost pass out when the stench hit you.

Despite our hatred for one another, at some moments, my brother and I only had each other. It's complicated. In the worst moments of my mom's rage, we were basically two kids huddled together in a corner, weathering the storm. There was a kind of unspoken mutual understanding between us in that, for better or worse, we always knew we had each other. Dealing with my mom certainly would've been even scarier as an only child. I always felt an odd sense of protection, because my brother and I were in it together. If it ever came down to a life-and-death situation, I know my brother and I would've dropped our mutual hatred and somehow fought through.

Our most turbulent years as brother and sister were at age six and below. As we got into our preteen years, some semblance of a relationship started to grow. Back in Indiana, we even had shared friends, mostly from our performing arts school. And when we first moved to Colorado, there was initially a sense of shared knowledge that we were in it together. That camaraderie lasted through the rest of that summer and into the first part of my awkward freshman year.

Then, as I started to find my feet socially, he started going down a darker path, and our relationship fell right back apart. By the time we were both working at King Soopers, we didn't even want to be affiliated with one another. We were completely opposed to what the other stood for and didn't want so much as to be mentioned in the same sentence. By the time I bought the family car, we didn't even carpool. I drove to work; he took the bus.

While all this was going on, my parents were so hard on him, partly because I got straight As and he didn't. Before high school ended, he ultimately had to repeat a grade. By that time, I was firmly established on the pom squad, hanging out with football players, and rapidly ascending the social pyramid, as my brother was coming to school wearing trench coats, painting his nails black, and generally radiating depression.

Our townhome was without much in the way of common space, so when friends came over, we'd just cram our separate friend groups in our own bedrooms. When the weather was nice, we could escape to the backyard, and our neighborhood also had a small clubhouse we could retreat to for a little more space.

Other times, especially when the weather was cold, one of us would inevitably take over the living room with our friends. If my friends were spread out over the floor and couches and one of his friends showed up, they'd have to walk over and through us to get to my brother's bedroom.

His friends would usually show up in full black goth makeup, wearing black trench coats and boots. The whole room would just go silent, and everyone avoided making eye contact. Then, as soon as whoever it was had made it through my group, shut the door, and disappeared into my brother's room, the whole living room would just explode into laughter. I'm sure they felt the exact same way about us when the reverse scenario happened.

The more I moved into the so-called cool crowd, the more I tried to fit in, and the more I tried to fit in, the more I started to get into trouble. I snuck out frequently to go to parties—just to *be there*. I thought I was so smart, living my "double life." I was fully supporting myself and a straight-A student, so even if I did get caught, I couldn't see how my parents could justify being upset. By that point, they weren't even really parenting or raising me. Of course, it didn't stop my mom from saying hateful things to me in passing.

Amanda, of course, showed me the way. I figured out how to tiptoe downstairs when everyone was asleep and creep out the back sliding door, where she and her older friends would be waiting in the car. By that time, we were spending every waking hour together, taking buses to big public pools, running around in our provocative clothes without any supervision. I'm grateful that nothing bad ever happened to us. Of course, she taught me how to flirt with boys. I could see how they looked at her, and it was appealing to me. I wasn't getting much love at home, and it was an easy fix to just put on some short shorts, bat my eyelashes, and get some boy's attention.

I was smart enough to never drink or do drugs—sneaking out was one thing, getting a drinking ticket was entirely another. I'd already been at parties that got busted and watched my friends get alcohol tickets, and I always got off because I was sober. My

Trouble inevitably caught up with us anyway.

strategy was to hang out with a full cup of alcohol while pretending to drink it; then I'd periodically go to the bathroom to dump it partly down the drain.

Trouble inevitably caught up with us anyway. One night I told my parents I was going to babysit, then went with my friends to a club in downtown Denver called Rock Island that had a sixteen-and-up night. I still wasn't drinking or doing drugs, but we did stay out past midnight in defiance of Denver's curfew. We left the club just before midnight and stopped at a gas station—we'd been dancing and having a great time, so we were all thirsty.

When my friends went in to get some water, there were police lingering outside, and they questioned my friends as soon as they came out. The cops ran my friends' IDs and arrested all of them, then came back to the car where I was waiting and arrested me too. They piled us all into the back of an eleven-passenger van, took us to the juvenile detention center, booked us, then made us sit there for two hours before calling our parents. We'd been arrested right after midnight, but they waited until it was much later to make it look worse.

I knew it was the end for me, and I was ultimately grounded for about a year, including on my seventeenth birthday. Of course, this felt like an absolute joke—I was still supporting myself and making perfect grades. Meanwhile, my mom was still in a drunken stupor every day, and my dad was in a perpetual state of depression, never talking to anyone or doing much of anything. By this time, both my parents were obese and generally not taking care of themselves.

Nevertheless, I played the game. I was still scared to death of my mom's wrath. I at least had a cell phone by then and was still able to start another job to save for college. I was still working at King Soopers, and on top of that, I started waitressing at an Indian restaurant a few doors down. Despite being grounded, I was still saving money and continued to excel in hip-hop and break dancing, and our pom squad was very good—we ultimately ranked third in the state.

By the time I was a senior in high school, I'd also met my high school sweetheart at one of the parties I'd snuck out to. His name was Bryan, and I was immediately drawn to him—not only was he good looking, laid back, and kind, but he wasn't like the other ego-driven high school boys who partied and played the field. He was a good, sweet boy, calm and simple, and that drew me to him. He wore Acqua di Gio cologne, and to this day, whenever I smell that cologne on someone, I still think of him.

He was the first guy that really, genuinely loved me. We had a wonderful relationship and were madly in love with one another. He went to a different school, had a good family, and had come from a solid blue-collar upbringing. He was very kind and respectful to me, and it was a beautiful relationship. After growing up with so much toxicity and abuse, finding a seminormal relationship was amazing.

In the end, high school was ultimately a positive experience. I'd transcended my awkward stage, earned the respect of a lot of my classmates, and graduated with a 4.2 GPA, which put me in the top 10 percent of my class. Toward the end of that year, I applied for a scholarship to University of Colorado Boulder and got it. My life seemed to be coming together, and I was so ready to finally get out of my house and away from my parents. I was so proud of myself for going from that big top in our yard in Valparaiso to what looked like a bright future.

Of course, my relationship with my mom was still rocky. There were spurts where she tried to turn it around and be present. She lost weight on the Atkins diet, and even came with my dad to almost all my football games when I was on the pom squad. She'd sneak in a water bottle full of vodka, but she tried. All the while, the more I was around different people, the more I realized that she and our family weren't normal. I saw how other people's moms didn't hate them, weren't nasty or derogatory, and didn't yell or scream or call them names.

On my eighteenth birthday, I got a tattoo of my name in Greek on my lower back. I'm named after my *yiayia*—my dad's mom, Mary, or *Maria* in Greek. My dad even helped me draw it. My mom had always said that none of her children would ever have a tattoo while living under her roof, but I was still supporting myself and paying rent, so the confident side of me didn't care if I got kicked out.

By that point, I was barely staying at my parents' house—once I turned eighteen, I was mostly staying with my boyfriend and at my friends' houses. When I came home and showed my mom the tattoo, she stopped talking to me for months. She told me she never wanted to see it, and whenever I was home, I had to keep it covered. Meanwhile, she continued to curse like a sailor around the clock.

My parents were still poor, partly from being so irresponsible with their money. My mom would rack up credit card debt on things that she absolutely did not need, whether it was movies, video games, takeout, or more and more alcohol. We couldn't so much as order a pizza without calling the number on the back of the credit card to see if we still had money available. She was continually opening new credit cards and maxing them out, talking about how poor we were and how unfair and unfortunate it all was.

The owners of the Indian restaurant I worked at knew our situation, and they'd always pack me bags of leftover food to take home. They were so kind and gracious and basically fed my family for a year without ever charging me. They even let my parents come in and eat at the restaurant. One night, a month or so after I got my tattoo, they came in and sat down in my section. When I came up to take their order, my mom, still refusing to talk to me on account of the tattoo, ordered through my dad. Classy. I hope she enjoyed her free meals.

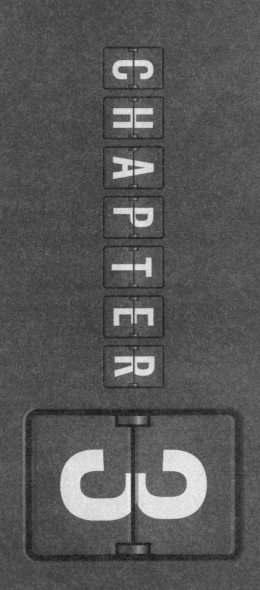

CHAPTER 3

CHAPTER 3

Toward the end of my senior year, my parents bought an older ranch house in Broomfield, a town not far outside of Boulder. It pushed them to the brink in terms of being able to afford it, but it was a nice rebound and a dream fulfilled for them after filing for bankruptcy and losing everything four years prior. I continued to be home less and less—it was still always nicer to stay with friends or my boyfriend. I was so excited to graduate and was dedicatedly saving up to get my own place or stay on campus once I started at the University of Colorado in the fall.

On the morning of April 24, 2002, I packed up my car with some personal items to move to the new house. Since my classes that semester didn't start until noon, I figured I'd go up there in the morning before heading to school. I left the townhouse we were moving out of and got onto Highway 36, which connects Boulder to Broomfield. This wasn't a typical route for me—almost all my driving up to that point had been confined to the city limits of Boulder: work, school, dance, home, my friends', and my boyfriend's, with a few side trips to the mall or the movie theater. If I did drive on the highway, it wasn't during rush hour.

I was in a great mood. I had the radio blasting, was singing at the top of my lungs, and was so in love with my high school sweetheart.

I had a pink fuzzy steering wheel, and in the center I had a picture of us that I'd printed out and stuck there with Scotch tape, right where you'd press to honk the horn.

It was rush hour, and I was rapidly accelerating onto the on-ramp to enter the highway. Not far after the merging lane ended, the highway came to a complete stop, which I was not anticipating. As I went to merge, I suddenly saw stalled traffic ahead of me. I started to panic, because I was still on the ramp pushing sixty-five.

I realized that I needed to slow down *and* move over a lane because the traffic was so deeply backed up in front of me. I failed to check the blind spot to my left, and when I tried to change lanes, the car there honked at me. I jerked the wheel away, lost control of the car, fishtailed, and spun out of control. I swerved to the right, then jerked to the left, shot across three or four lanes of traffic, then smashed into the concrete wall at the median. I wish there was drone footage of it—to this day, I cannot conceive of how I failed to hit or injure anyone else. That highway was absolutely packed. This is one example of how I know we have a loving God.

When I came to a stop, the dust from the airbag made it difficult to see inside the car. Thankfully, I'd been wearing my seat belt. The engine was smoking, and the radio was still blasting "I'm Real," by J-Lo and Ja Rule. Blood was running down my face, and I had contusions and airbag burns from the side of my hands and up my wrists.

The smoke made me think the car was on fire. My driver's-side door was smashed and wouldn't open, so I started to crawl to the other side of the car to escape out the passenger-side door. Some good Samaritans had pulled over, and they helped pull me out through the passenger side. I walked away from the wreck holding on to them, then sat on the ground and waited for the ambulance—it would be the last time I'd walk for some time.

When the adrenaline finally subsided, I knew I was going to be in so much trouble, because it was *my fault*. When the paramedics arrived, I lied and said I didn't have any injuries. I was scared to go to the hospital—I did *not* want to pay those bills. I was still supporting myself and wasn't making more than $800 or $900 a month. My scholarship to CU Boulder was only partial, and I knew my expenses were going to be increasing, so I was *not* trying to pay for an ambulance ride.

Meanwhile, my brother had been driving at the exact same time on the same highway, but in the other direction. He passed the scene, saw my car from across the road, and immediately went to get my mom, because she worked right off the interchange nearby. Eventually, my dad made it down too.

As awful as my upbringing was, my parents were still my parents. I was in pain and had just had a very traumatic experience. Any little girl at that moment would want to have parents there, to fall into their arms and have a safe place to be, but I just could not get that from my mom. She immediately started in with how I'd wrecked the car, how much it would cost, and how the insurance would go up. My dad, at least, seemed to be a little bit more caring and comforting.

From there, they took me to the hospital and through the ER. As the adrenaline continued to wear off, I realized two things: how much pain I was in and that I *really* couldn't walk. Thankfully, I didn't have any broken bones, but there were torn ligaments in my lower back that the doctors wanted to repair through physical therapy. I'd hurt my left shoulder and right hip and had a concussion, and my neck was a mess. The bruising was bad, and I still had cuts all over my face, but I thankfully didn't need surgery or stitches.

I knew from the second I spoke to the doctors that dancing would not be in my future for a long time. I was optimistic that I could still attend college, but muscle damage and torn ligaments take a long time to heal. When I got home, I laid down on the couch and replayed the tape of the accident over and over in my mind. *What did I just do?* The guilt, shame, and embarrassment were overwhelming.

When the police showed up at the scene of the accident, I'd made up a story on the spot to try to get myself out of a ticket. I told them I'd been cut off while merging, panicked, slammed on my brakes, and lost control. They'd given me a ticket anyway, probably because there were other witnesses whose testimonies contradicted my own.

I simply couldn't bear the weight of blaming myself on top of everything that I'd lost.

I've been lying about this story ever since. I told it to myself and to others so much that I just started believing the lie. I simply couldn't bear the weight of blaming myself on top of everything that I'd lost. This accident was twenty years ago, and in finally telling it here, I've at last forgiven myself. This accident was my fault, and it cost me what I thought, at that point, was everything.

I was one month away from breaking free of my parents, graduating from high school, living on my own, taking care of myself, and starting a future on my own terms. I'd poured my entire life into dance, and the crash resulted in me losing my entire identity as a dancer. It completely altered who I was, the path I was on, what I was going to do with my life—my escape, my talent, my everything.

At this point, through the good grace of God, I can finally forgive myself. He has led me down an unbelievable path—one that's led to a situation where I have a platform to share this story with anyone who's been through something similar. Now that I've forgiven myself, I finally feel comfortable telling the truth, but for a long time after the accident, I was just so ashamed.

I also had no plan B. To make matters worse, my dad lost his job shortly thereafter—there was a claim filed against him for sexually harassing a coworker, and he got fired. He was stuck at home on unemployment, and my mom was still working her minimum-wage job. They had *just* bought their new house, so the timing was very, very bad. My brother and I were still helping out and paying rent, but not being able to work also chipped away at the shred of identity I had left. I only had a small savings account. I started to doubt whether I'd even be able to go to college in the fall.

Fear rushed in, and I didn't have any faith to lean on back then. I didn't know anything about Jesus, so I thought that in order to survive, it 100 percent depended on me. Without faith or a supportive family, plans A, B, and C started and ended with Mary. Thankfully, I was able to file a short-term disability workers' compensation claim, which provided 60 percent of my wages while I was healing from the accident. Because taxes don't come out of that, that 60 percent was close to what I'd been taking home. I was so grateful for that.

And in the end, I was and am a strong girl—I'm brave, I'm bold, and I'm a fighter. I fought through all my physical therapy appointments and did everything the doctors recommended. I was deeply committed to regaining the strength of my body and eventually got to the point where I could walk, go up and down stairs, and even drive again.

In the meantime, since he had nothing better to do, my dad was taking me to all my appointments. All the while, my mom talked down to him, just like she did with the rest of us. At that point, he did what he was told to do—he was beat down to a point that he didn't have a voice whatsoever in the household. My mom ran the show, and he was treated like an accessory.

After years of being so busy and always away from the house, I now found myself stuck at home with my dad in mutual utter misery. It was the first time since childhood that I'd spent much time with him, and that broke my heart. Losing your job for sexual harassment makes it difficult to get hired anywhere else, and I'm sure it wasn't easy for him to see his overachieving daughter who'd had the world at her fingertips laid up right next to him.

Back in Indiana, I used to look up to him so much. He was one of the best opera singers I've ever heard, and of my two parents, he was always the warmest and kindest to me. I almost had a good run at daddy's little girl, but he had his own demons, and moreover, my mom was jealous of our relationship. She couldn't stand that he seemed to like me more than her. We were both afraid to show any sort of love for one another in front of her, because she'd instantly get jealous and start in on both of us.

Because of my dad's history of sexual indiscretions, she gradually started thinking that he was abusing me, which wasn't the case. Nevertheless, she would just lay into him, which would make things even worse. It was so sad to see my dad in that state. He had been an accomplished opera singer and actor, appeared in dozens of movies, and even performed in Chicago with the likes of Chris Farley. Deep down, he really was a true artist. Growing up, I'd always seen him in the bright lights, the star of every production he was in. Now, he'd become an overweight, miserable bump on a log whose whole life, purpose, and meaning were long gone, and that broke my heart.

My sisters knew how rough it'd been for me, so they flew out to see me the night before my graduation party. Of course, given everyone's relationship with my mom, we kept it a secret. I snuck over to see them at their hotel, and we had an amazing time.

At my party the next day, I attempted to act surprised when they walked through the door. It's still hard for me to lie to this day, and because we were lying to my mom, my fear made it even worse. I'm sure she could tell I was lying through my teeth. Her feelings were clearly hurt, and she proceeded to drink her way through the party.

My sisters didn't stay long—by the next morning, they were gone. On one hand, it was such a special moment for which I was so grateful, and it really cheered me up. On the other, it continued to drive even more of a wedge between my mom and me. After all, my sisters got to leave town, and I was still trapped in the house, dealing with her wrath.

After months of physical therapy, I finally was in a place where I could think about starting college. I made it to my orientation, and it was so hard to walk around campus. My body had simply not healed. CU Boulder is a huge campus. My little injured body was entirely unprepared, but I refused to fail.

I remember going into my first dance class. For the first time in so long, I had my leotard and tights on, but I had put on a lot of weight over the summer from the lack of movement. Before the wreck, I'd been dancing twenty to thirty hours a week while working at the restaurant. Then I'd spent months lying around on the couch all day eating cereal. I had no flexibility, my technique was out the window, and my back constantly hurt. Despite everything, I pushed my way through that first semester, lying to myself every day that I could do it, because at that point I'd never really failed in my life.

I was *still* waitressing, running around campus, *and* trying to dance. My teacher knew I was injured and gave me a bit of a pass but chose to grade me hard. I was still living at home, which of course was the absolute worst place for me to be. I just didn't have enough money at the time to get a space of my own—it was far cheaper to pay a couple hundred bucks a month to my parents than to get my own apartment.

As my first semester wore on, I came to hate my life. In losing my ability to dance at the level I once had, I'd lost my north star, and it put me in such a desperate state. I didn't know my way out of the problem, and it wore me down. I lost the passion and fire inside me. I'd had such a vision to become a professional dancer, and now merely walking around campus all day and then waitressing at night was a struggle.

For the first time in my life, my grades suffered. The university put me on academic probation. Meanwhile, I'd broken a small test tube in a chemistry class—I think they cost eleven cents. Crazily, through some quirk of academic bureaucracy, that outstanding balance of eleven cents *also* prevented me from registering for classes. Finally, over Christmas break, I just said, *To heck with this*, and dropped out.

I had never quit anything in my life at that point. I had just turned nineteen, and I realized that I increasingly didn't know who I was or what was even good about me anymore. The only positive thing remaining in my life was my boyfriend and his family. They loved me, and he was my safe harbor. It was really the first time I

My number one goal was still to save up enough money to get out of my parents' house for good.

had experienced consistent love in my life, because I never got it from my parents.

Bryan was all that I had. He was so good to me, but because I had never really experienced that kind of healthy love, I didn't quite know what to do with it. Deep inside me, I think there was a fear, rooted in my upbringing, that kept whispering, *It won't last*. It was a protective mechanism—I was scared to fall as hard as I could have.

Once I'd dropped out, I knew I'd have to grow up and get at least one real full-time job. My number one goal was still to save up enough money to get out of my parents' house for good, but I had no idea how I was going to do it. I briefly considered teaching dance, but I still wasn't sufficiently recovered.

At the time, I sometimes went to a nail and tanning salon by our house, and there one day a beautiful woman with long blond hair struck up a conversation with me. The second I walked in, she started complimenting me, telling me how beautiful I was. Her name was Tara, and she had all kinds of questions: *How old are you? What's your story? What do you do? Where do you live?*

I was still broken. I didn't think I was pretty enough or that I had anything going for me, and on top of that, I had just lost my entire future and identity as a performing artist.

Growing up, my parents and brother were not very complimentary of me. I was the laughingstock of our family. They mostly tended to make fun of me any time we sat down to eat as a family. I hate to repeat it, but they called me "the retarded one," and I was the center of every joke. I had been beaten down my entire life and didn't know my worth. I was now in the worst state I'd ever been in, and I felt I had no purpose in my life. The only plan I had was to make money and break free from my family.

Tara asked if I'd ever thought about dancing for a living. I told her I had been on track to become a professional dancer until the accident. To this she said, "That's not the kind of dancing I'm talking about."

She started talking about go-go dancing in nightclubs, and even exotic dancing. I had never been exposed to those types of things. I was raised on my parents' inappropriate R-rated movies, but I had never, ever been to one of those types of clubs. At the time, I wasn't even twenty-one.

She said I should come down and audition at the club she worked at. "We make so much money—you could make $1,000 in a week." Well, that got my attention: *$1,000 a week? I could buy a house with that kind of money!* She coached me a little bit, told me what to bring, what to wear.

I ultimately went down to the club in Denver to audition, and walking into the place gave me the absolute worst feeling of my life. I got up on their stage, and though I was still injured, I found that kind of dancing is a walk in the park compared to the kind of competitive dance I'd been doing.

In the end, the manager wanted to hire me. I never in a million years would have seen myself in that kind of environment, but my thought process was, *If this is what it will take for me to make some money fast, just for a season, so I can get out on my own, find a place, buy a new car, and become self-sufficient, then I'm in.*

When I told my boyfriend, he was disappointed, and I don't blame him. It led to our breakup, which, of course, was devastating to me. He was my rock, my everything. At that point, I really didn't know who I was without him. When I lost him, I lost the last good thing in my life. And with that, I entered the darkest season of my entire existence.

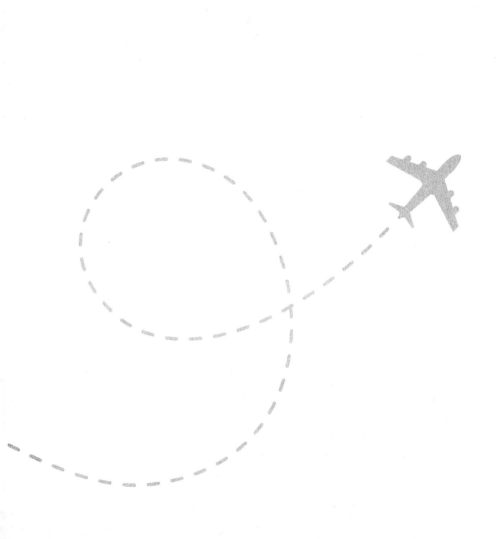

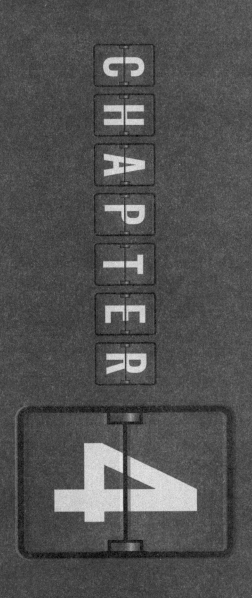

CHAPTER

4

CHAPTER 4

I've never told anyone about this chapter of my life. Again, I only feel empowered to share this story because I've forgiven myself, and I know that there are other women out there who have made similarly poor choices and *haven't* forgiven themselves. Christ redeems and restores. God has forgiven me. I've repented and completely changed my life. Sometimes, when we're in tough situations, we do the best that we can with what we have at our disposal. In the end, I made the best decision that I could have at the time.

Despite my heartbreak over my high school sweetheart, I felt like I was going to keep my head on straight. I resolved to not get into the dark, scary side of the business and only stay there for a couple of months. I just needed to make money, build up a nest egg, and then get another restaurant job. I can *almost* even say that I'm proud of myself, because that's *almost* what I did.

I kept a good conscience and kept my head on straight, but it took a little bit longer to get out than I'd initially hoped. For young women that grow up in abusive, alcoholic families, this type of profession is oddly comfortable for them. So many come from the same kind of broken childhood that I did. I was nineteen, lying about my age, and making the wrong kinds of friends.

There was a restaurant and bar next door, and the workers knew very well that most of us were underage, but they still let us hang out until dawn. When they'd close at two in the morning, we'd hide in the bathrooms until the rest of the regular patrons left and reemerge when they locked the doors behind them. There, we'd continue partying for the rest of the night, drinking Red Bull and vodka, doing cocaine, and singing karaoke until dawn. The night bartender would eventually leave, the morning crew would roll in, reopen, and make the best breakfast burritos. I'd wolf one of those down, drive home, take a NyQuil, sleep away the day, then go straight back to the club in the afternoon.

Even though I got sucked into the dark side of the business with the drugs and the drinking, I was still very good at saving my money.

I was soon making well over $1,000 a week and wanted to be as responsible with that money as possible. Even though I got sucked into the dark side of the business with the drugs and the drinking, I was still very good at saving my money. I only had to work at that place for a month before I had enough money to live on my own.

Finally, I rented my own apartment. My mom was upset when I moved out. As usual, she was in a drunken stupor. She was stomping around the house, finding things that were mine, then throwing them at the movers I'd hired. I was used to this kind of behavior from her behind closed doors, but it was so embarrassing to see her like that in front of other people.

When I was finally settled in my new apartment, I felt amazing finally having my own space. My thoughts quieted. I finally felt like I wasn't surrounded by demons. I could decorate it the way I wanted to, even though it was mostly with cheap furniture from Walmart.

I had a wire-frame futon in the living room with awkward cushions on top, but it was *mine*, and I was proud of it. I was proud of myself for doing what I needed to do to break away from my toxic family.

Back at home, they were in bad shape. My dad's car had broken down multiple times. Once, it had even left him stranded in a snowstorm, and he still didn't have the money to fix it. I felt bad for him, and since I was making so much money, I wanted to give him a present. I found an older clean white Ford F-150 on Craigslist, bought it for $3,000 in cash, drove it to the house, put a big red bow on it, and left it in the driveway. I was so proud of myself for helping my dad, and I think he was surprised that I would do something like that for him.

Then, immediately, my mom realized, *Wait a second. Mary apparently makes a lot of money now. This is an income source we can tap into.* They didn't know what I did for work. I'd told them I was teaching dance in Denver on top of another part-time job. Instantly, my mom turned on the charm and started playing a new role. *Actually, I really like you. In fact, I love you. You're wonderful and amazing. And, by the way, we're three months behind on our energy and gas bills and two weeks late on our mortgage. We don't want to lose the house. Is there any way you can help us out?*

At this point, maybe you'd think I'd be strong enough to say, *No, lady, you're a mean witch, and you can't take anything more from me.* But in a way, this was the moment I'd waited for my entire life. Maybe, I thought, she would finally find value in me. Maybe I could bring value into her life. I could be her knight in shining armor. She'd been waiting *her* whole life to have someone who would bless her rather than harm her, and I saw an opportunity to be that person. I didn't think this explicitly, but deep down, it came down to something like, *Maybe I can buy my mom's love.*

In practice, it was more like, *Maybe I can use this extra money to better my mom's life. Then, maybe—just maybe—she'll turn everything around.* And with that, I took on the role of financially supporting my parents. Instantly, they were so nice to me. *So* nice. And of course, it was all a performance, something they were highly trained to do.

Meanwhile, there was a regular patron at my work to whom I took a liking; it was mutual, and we started dating. He was ten years older than me and had a good job, making roughly $80,000 per year. Of course, the first thing that he wanted me to do was to quit working there because he was jealous. I said OK, quit, and got a job at Hooters. This was *his* recommendation—he and his friends went there every Sunday. They all just loved eating wings, drinking beer, and watching football.

As you can imagine, my income dropped. I'd been making thousands and thousands of dollars per month, then went back down to a normal waitress's wage. Soon, I had to tell my parents that I was changing jobs and didn't have the income I'd had before so I couldn't extend the financial support they'd quickly gotten used to.

Guess what happened next? Like a light switch, they went back to treating me exactly like they always had, and it broke my heart. I realized that I'd been taken advantage of and that I had been buying their love. The moment that the well dried up, their "love" was gone, and though I should have seen it coming, it was still devastating to me.

I entered another state of depression. With my income slashed significantly, I was back in my old struggle. I'd had an awesome savings account going, but I had extended the majority of that to help my parents. Then my boyfriend started to become more and more controlling. He demanded that I move into his house. He wasn't comfortable with me living thirty minutes away, though I was already staying at his house a few nights a week. When my lease ended, I let go of my apartment and did just that.

At home, he drank beer constantly. There was beer in the fridge in the garage, and more beer in the fridge inside the house. Whenever we got home, he didn't even wait to get inside—after we'd park in the garage, he'd go into the garage fridge, crack one open, and have a sip before he even walked into the house. He was overweight from all the beer and fried food—we had a FryDaddy in the house, and he'd start the day by making and eating fried jalapeño poppers and chicken fingers for breakfast. I inevitably put on weight living in that environment too.

Because he ate so poorly, he suffered from extreme acid reflux. It would kick up every night like clockwork, so he'd go into the bathroom to throw up. Because there was always vomit everywhere in the bathroom, he'd just pull the door shut instead of cleaning it. The smell was so horrible that I refused to go in. It was hard to even *look*—on top of the vomit, there were beard clippings always scattered everywhere.

Fortunately, we had separate bathrooms. One of the first things I did upon moving in was to get a wire scrubber and bleach, because the bottom of *my* bathtub was *black*. He never lifted a finger to clean anything, so I became the one responsible for cleaning the house. It was quite a lot of work—he had a rottweiler that shed profusely and left huge piles of poop everywhere. My boyfriend would never clean it up, so before I came around, it would just sit there and accumulate, mostly in the basement and on the basement stairs. Instead of going so far as to clean the basement, I just avoided it entirely.

We both smoked cigarettes at the time. I was following right in my parents' footsteps: drinking, smoking, eating unhealthy food, living among pet accidents all over the house. My boyfriend was cut right from the same cloth, but the nature of his abuse was different. Soon, he decided to start controlling when I was or wasn't at home, when I got to see my friends, and finally, where I was in general. It would only get worse from there.

I decided on my own that I was done working at Hooters—there was too much drama among the girls there, and besides, I wanted to go get a real bartending or waitressing job to make more money. I left Hooters for a bar called Patrick's, where I started cocktail waitressing in the pool room. On Fridays and Saturdays, they had live music, and while I did start to make more money, I was working late. I would get home at three or later in the morning and sleep through most of the next day.

As you might expect, my boyfriend didn't love those hours. In no time at all, he was on to the next step: engagement and marriage. When he proposed on my twenty-first birthday, I said yes. We planned to get married nine months later, over Labor Day weekend. Over the next ten months, despite the profound difference in our incomes, he never offered to pay for any of it. Though we were living together, he still insisted on keeping our bills separate. I started working all sorts of extra part-time jobs, doing anything I could to be able to pay for the wedding. I started selling cosmetics through Mary Kay and even became a biker babe for a motorcycle website.

I was figuring out how to operate independently.

My parents still had next to nothing, and I wasn't making much money, but everything else related to the wedding was still on me. I managed to find us a location at a Victorian house in the town of Golden. It had a large dining hall and nice little area outside where you could get married, but in the end it was just a step above a backyard wedding.

The lead-up to the event was, of course, tumultuous. By that time, I'd been living away from my parents for almost three years, but our relationship remained strained. I was still under their spell of manipulation and control. I was trying to earn their love through money while simultaneously trying to separate myself from them, still struggling to assert myself but too scared to fully stand up to my mom. I was figuring out how to operate independently, starting to feel more like an adult, and at least asserting some control over what I wanted to be a part of—or not.

I wanted my dad to sing at the wedding, but he said he wasn't comfortable performing after so many years out of practice. He simply wasn't ready to bring his talent out of the closet and resurrect it in front of friends and family. He was still in such a dark place, and by letting his talent slip away, he lost hold of the one thing he loved the most. On top of everything else, I still think he felt like a failure for losing the school. In the end, I ultimately hired a string quartet.

Every girl wants her mom's help in planning her wedding, and despite everything, I was no exception. For those nine months, I desperately tried to have a moment when I felt like I had a mom who loved me and that planning my wedding was something special. She *did* agree to host my bridal shower—in the end, she was a traditionalist and insisted upon it—and I *do* think, deep down, it was important to her. I know she made sure everyone at work knew her daughter was getting married. She threw the bridal shower in the basement of her home and invited a ton of people that she knew, and I invited a select few friends.

At that point, everything started to become real. It very rapidly dawned on me that I was knowingly about to enter another toxic, abusive relationship, just like the one I was struggling to escape with my parents, but this time with a horrible man. At the same time, I felt like I was so far down the path that I couldn't turn back. Suddenly, I felt trapped and knew beyond a doubt I was making a horrible mistake. Looking around at all the people who had shown up with gifts made it so much worse. I ultimately locked myself in the bathroom in the middle of the party, hyperventilating and crying from sheer panic brought on by the horrible decision I was making.

Of all people, the one who was able to help me through was my brother, who was still living with my parents. He heard me crying through the door, tapped on it, and asked me to let him in. He brought in a pair of headphones, put them on my head, played some music, and generally tried to calm me down. It's one of the nicest things he ever did for me.

When he tried to talk me through it, I told him I felt like I was too young to get married, was making a mistake, and that my fiancé wasn't the right person for me but that I was in too deep. I just wasn't ready to stand up—for myself, to my mom, *or* to my fiancé. I blamed myself for letting things go too far and felt like it was my responsibility to deal with the consequences. My line of thought was, *I got myself into the mess, and now I have to deal with it.*

My brother was able to calm me down enough to rejoin the party, but I was numb for the rest of the day. All these people had shown up with wonderful gifts, and each time I opened one, I felt more and more guilty. I felt deeply sorry that people had spent their money to shower me for what I knew was about to be a huge mistake. Afterward, I took all the gifts home and just stacked them in the corner of the poop-filled basement—I didn't want to open or even look at them, so I just let them sit there.

Things didn't get much better from there. I continued trying to plan things without a clue or any guidance as to what I was doing. I particularly didn't know it's the bride-to-be's responsibility to plan an itinerary for out-of-state guests, block out a group of hotel rooms, arrange transportation and meals, et cetera. I was all of twenty-one. I simply had *no* idea.

The person that I upset the most by not having those kinds of plans in place was my mom's mom—this intensely buttoned-up terror of a woman who wore pink suits, pearls, heels, and pantyhose daily until the day she died. She spared no harsh words in conveying how inconsiderate I was to her and my other out-of-town guests, then laid into my mom, who of course laid into me. This all sent me further into my spiral of dread.

As the week of the wedding approached, I was distracting myself from reality by focusing on more logistics—I also hadn't known I was supposed to print out maps for everybody, make welcome kits, or suggest things to do. The whole process completely mystified me, but I worked to put everything together the best I could.

When my sisters came to town, I finally had a bit of reprieve. By that point, I was a nervous wreck, and I felt like I got to escape into their arms and rest for a moment. I was very upset and absolutely did not want to get married, but we stayed in a hotel the night before the wedding, and I managed to put on a good show.

My oldest sister is a beautician and a hair stylist, so when we got up the next morning, she helped me with my hair and makeup and getting dressed. As we were just about ready to head to the venue, we saw my mom carrying around her water bottle, which was filled with pure vodka.

By the time we arrived at the venue, she was drunk, making a scene and generally being her usual charming self—that's a joke. It was hot that day, and the temperature was climbing into the nineties. The main tack she took for my wedding day was saying things like,

"Who chooses to get married outside over Labor Day weekend in the dead of summer? Couldn't you have thought this through?"

To make matters worse, I was getting married in Heritage Square, which is filled with cute little restaurants and shops. In the summer there's often a merry-go-round and Ferris wheel set up and an open space in the middle of the square where bands play. A cover band had set up during our wedding, and by the time we were exchanging vows, they had gone into a spirited rendition of "Mustang Sally." My mom thought that was trashy and wasn't afraid to share her opinion with everyone. By the time we had to take family pictures, she had turned into Attila the Hun, adamantly directing everyone, including the photographer.

Next, we were ushered into the basement of the venue, where a priest was waiting with pens to sign the marriage license. I went down there praying that I could somehow not sign it, "forget" to sign it, remove it, throw it away—anything so that the marriage wouldn't be official or legal. The photographer wanted to take pictures, and I remember not wanting to submit to that additional bit of proof either. My heart was broken, and I couldn't believe what I was getting myself into, but I ended up signing it anyway. In my mind, I rationalized everything by telling myself I'd just hide it, shred it, say I lost it.

From there, we proceeded to the reception. When we sat down after being welcomed as bride and groom, my mom headed straight over to yell in my face in front of everyone. *We need to serve food. You're holding up dinner. Our out-of-town guests are starving.* She was so hammered by that point that I doubt she remembers any of it. The evening had been thoroughly ruined by that point, and I was just doing my best to get through it.

By the time everyone left, we went back to our hotel room, where it was time for "our big wedding night." There, my husband went back into his familiar routine from home: proceeding straight to the bathroom with his acid reflux to spend the remainder of the night vomiting. Meanwhile, I curled myself into a ball in the bed and went to sleep, hoping things would be different in the morning. Of course, they weren't. When the sun rose, I woke up married.

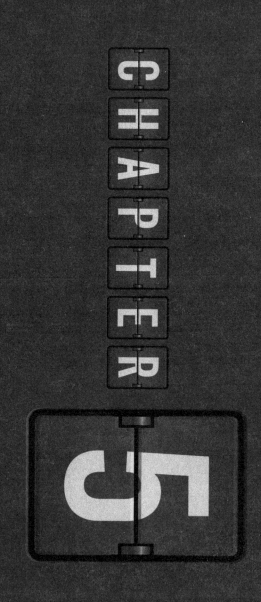

CHAPTER 5

CHAPTER 5

My husband made clear that I was not to take on any further nightlife jobs and that I needed to find an eight-to-five posthaste. I went to a staffing agency, and they placed me in a part-time receptionist position at a mortgage company right by where my husband worked. He purposely helped select the opportunity and location so we could carpool there and back.

Unfortunately, that was an eleven-dollars-per-hour job, and because I wasn't even putting in forty hours a week, I wasn't making enough money to survive. Meanwhile, we still had separate bank accounts. At that point, my husband was making close to $90,000 a year yet sharing none of it. We still split the check at dinner and continued to handle our expenses separately. I had no money for anything and was definitely not ready to have kids, so I resolved to start looking for a different job.

I looked in the newspaper and saw a forty-hour-a-week job at a payroll company we'll call PayCo, starting at thirteen dollars an hour. That jump in income would take me to $29,000 a year in earnings. I went out and bought a suit I couldn't afford at Kohl's for the interview and kept the tags on so I could return it.

My first screening interview was with a girl named Jessica. She was interviewing for her replacement—the position I wanted—as she was being promoted to the small-business sales team. After she moved me forward, I met my future manager. He was a successful, well-spoken thirtysomething man in a beautiful suit, and he was running the company's number one sales team in the entire country.

When I looked around at the other people working in the office, they all looked equally impressive. I had no degree and a few short months working as a receptionist to my name. I'd been working in the service industry, was mixed up with people doing drugs, and was married to a disgusting, controlling slob. It was certainly a jarring change of pace.

My new manager saw something in me that I had never seen in myself.

From the second I walked into that office, I instantly felt like it was going to be my home for a long time. Somehow, it just felt like I'd have a future there. It felt safe and bright and light. Just being there made me feel a new inner sense of peace, despite how underqualified I felt. Somehow, I knew that my life was about to change forever, and in the end, I wasn't wrong.

My new manager saw something in me that I had never seen in myself. The interview process was fast, and when I found out I got the job, I could barely believe it. Somehow I knew it would be a turning point in my life. For five days a week, it gave me the opportunity to get away from that disgusting house and my toxic relationship. Even though the pay was only a little bit more per hour, it was just enough to cover my living expenses, and I knew if I got a raise, I'd be doing okay.

On the other hand, my husband was not pleased, because it forced him to give up a sliver of control. Plus, we wouldn't be carpooling anymore. PayCo was a seven-minute 4.3-mile straight-shot drive down Airport Road from our house, and there were train tracks on the way. Whenever I was stopped by a train and it made me even a few minutes late, my husband would be waiting there in the garage, standing by his beer fridge, smoking a cigarette, seething.

Even if I pulled in at 5:08 p.m., he'd ask where I'd been and what took me so long, and over and over again, I'd be deeply apologetic. *I'm so sorry. I left right on time. I saw the train coming, and I tried to go around it, but there was a car in front of me. I'm so sorry. I can try to call you in the future and let you know: "Hey, I'm stuck at the train tracks, so I'll be home ninety seconds later."* Then, for the rest of the night, he'd be short with me, avoiding eye contact, huffing, puffing, and generally making it very uncomfortable for me to be at home. It was very much like how I'd been raised, and I just took it.

I was under the spell of this man. He had the same control over me as my mom did—I gave both of them all my power, and they knew I was a puppet and that I wasn't ever going to speak up or stand up for myself. Like my mom, I lived in constant fear of upsetting my husband, and wanted to please him at all costs. I was always overcompensating for his bad attitude, doing whatever I could to brighten his day. In those days, I was a people pleaser in the worst way—I'd do whatever it took to make people like me, because I needed to be validated so I could feel self-worth.

But now I had a job to go to, and in the beginning, I was so nervous. On my first day I sat in my car in the parking lot until the clock struck 7:59 a.m. I felt so much pressure, but it was exciting pressure—I knew that this place was different, and that it was just what I needed in order to get my life on track.

When I finally went in, I found the onboarding process a bit overwhelming, but I got to set up a few things at my brand-new desk, then started my six weeks of training with Jessica. At first, I just tried to be a good student and listen attentively. It helped that she was a good teacher. Within a few days, it became clear that the role was a lot easier than she thought it was—or at least it felt like that to me. I picked up everything quickly, and after two weeks I felt fully trained. Soon it became a little annoying to have someone hovering around and monitoring me. When I told my new manager that I understood the job and didn't need another month of supervision, that did *not* sit well with Jessica—she thought I was just a *little* too sassy.

In my first few months working at the mortgage company, I was just sitting around answering the phone and sorting the mail. This was my first real corporate job, doing actual work, and I was so excited when it all came easily to me. Right out of the gate, I was ideating on better, more efficient ways of doing things, asking pointed questions, and generally picking things up fast.

For example, there was disorganized, duplicate-heavy data spread pointlessly across multiple spreadsheets—why don't we consolidate them? Jessica had been in that role for five years, and I think my arrival chipped at her ego a bit. She warned me against being overconfident, but after I talked to my manager, she backed off, and she only came back to help me sporadically from then on.

At the same time, I was all of twenty-two and still cursing like a sailor, just like my mom. I was also still smoking cigarettes and probably smelled like it, and obviously I was still poor—my work attire was not great. Coming from the service industry, I was still gossipy, and unwisely carried that into corporate life. My coworkers immediately took note of all of the above. They especially didn't like how much I instantly clicked with my manager.

I dealt with a lot of adversity starting out—there were a lot of within-earshot whispers of how I was too big for my britches, needed to take a seat, and should stop speaking up as if I was smarter than everyone else. And they were mostly right: I *was* the person that talked too much and always had an opinion, which, of course, I also got from my mom.

Nevertheless, I learned the ropes, mastered the administrative parts of my role, and proceeded to go way beyond the call of duty. When you sell payroll services and submit a new client to operations, a mountain of data comes along with it: federal and state tax documentation, tax ID numbers, filing frequency, payroll registers, bank information, and power of attorney documents. Learning to juggle all that was hugely beneficial down the road—new salespeople often struggle with the nuances of heavy paperwork and technical integrations. Learning all those unglamourous parts of the job eventually allowed me to take on more than my role required and helped me accelerate.

I was so fortunate in that my office was host to at least a dozen talented, top-performing women sales reps with so much going for them: married, amazing kids, nice cars, dressed to the nines, making great money, and thriving in their amazing careers. *Finally*, I thought. *A model of my future self. This is who and what I want to be.* I was so ready to start stepping into that role and believed that everything they had would soon be coming to me.

A couple of months into my new role, my manager was extremely pleased with me. He loved my work, thought I was the best assistant he'd ever had, and told me that I had a very bright future, provided I take it upon myself to go to school and get a degree. He told me that PayCo had a tuition reimbursement program and recommended that I do nighttime classes or an online program, because the company would pay for it.

All the while I was thinking, *This is unbelievable*. I was so excited, but when I went home to tell my husband, he laid a huge guilt trip on me. "Why would you do that? Why do you need to go to school? You're working full time. If you enroll in classes, it'll be on *our* time, when we're together. You're just going to leave me here by myself and ignore me so that you can go do *this*, when you don't even need to?"

I went back to my boss and told him I didn't think I could do it because my husband didn't approve. At that point, my manager started to pry a bit and asked about what my life was like at home. I started to confide in him and told him my story, which really opened his eyes—he realized he had a broken young woman in a bad situation on his hands.

Eventually I also told him about my toxic relationship with my parents and gradually found a safe place through confiding in him. In the process, he opened up to me about things in his life, too, whether the tragic loss of his mom or his career trajectory. As we started to learn more about one another, our relationship grew into a deep friendship. He became more and more encouraging with me, and when he gave me advice on what to do about my husband, a lot of it worked—the conversations I had at home with my husband were eerily similar to sales conversations and allowed me to get what I wanted without setting him off. More and more, I started to see my worth and became more confident in speaking up for myself.

Eventually, with my manager's help, I was able to enroll in school. I started to dedicate my weekends to studying. One thing I figured out very quickly was how to "CLEP" out of classes: you can buy a college textbook, pay a few hundred dollars, and take a CLEP exam for college credit, as long as you pass. I'd leave work on Friday, go to the library, study from a textbook all weekend long, get excused from work on Monday, then go on to ace my exams. I ultimately "CLEPed" out of the majority of my associate's degree, which saved me years and so much money.

With all those foundational credits under my belt, I used my tuition reimbursement from PayCo to finish out the last few credits of my associate's degree through the University of Phoenix. From there, I started a bachelor's program in accounting, business, and marketing. I learned a ton, *and* it was all immediately relevant to what I was doing at work—often, I was able to implement things I learned in class in real life the very next day. I knew I wanted to embark on a sales career, and my marketing courses were extremely helpful in preparing for that.

While I did very well academically, it was stressful to plow through all the classes at night after working a full day. The University of Phoenix conducted classes in a group-learning style—they'd assign four or five people to a project, and everybody would ultimately get the same grade. Sometimes my classmates' contributions were decent, but most of the time they were garbage. I'm type A and stubborn, and there was no way I

While I did very well academically, it was stressful to plow through all the classes at night after working a full day.

was going to accept a bad grade. Because I was usually the team leader, and knowing my grade was dependent on it, I would often redo everyone else's work. Over time, that became a heavy burden to bear.

I remember sitting there struggling with how difficult it was, crying, exhausted, not wanting to continue. The whole time, my manager was so encouraging and constantly reassuring me of my work's importance. My main motivation became to fulfill my promise to him and the company. Plus, back in 2006, a degree really meant something—you truly needed that piece of paper to advance in your career. Because I genuinely wanted to move up in the organization, I took the process seriously. In the end, I saw it through to completion and earned a 3.89 GPA.

As time passed, my manager's and my relationship continued to deepen. He genuinely cared about me, my well-being, and my success and continued to advise me on how to deal with my husband. Eventually, it became clear that I needed to get out of that house. Together, we constructed a plan: when I was already traveling to Vegas for work, I'd come back a day early, sneak into our house while he was at work, and move everything of mine out. I knew my husband would demand to see my itinerary, so I showed it to him before changing my flight to a day earlier.

On the big day, my manager, another manager, and I—all still in formal business attire—left work, got a moving truck, drove to the house, cleared out my stuff, and moved it into a new low-income apartment complex—it was only $600 per month and not in a good area, but it was just what I needed at the time. When everything was out, I left my husband a simple note: *I'm leaving you, and am filing for divorce.* I just walked away.

I didn't have enough money at the time to pay for the attorneys, so my manager helped me to cover the initial cost to get the divorce filings underway. It was such a huge blessing to get out of that marriage. In the end, I didn't ask for anything—no money, nor equity on that disgusting house. I just wanted to be gone, safe, and protected.

And as soon as I got out of that house, everything changed for me. I realized that I had a great job and worked with great people, and I started to clearly see what my life could look like. I still needed to make some extra money, because I was fully supporting myself again. I got a part-time job teaching dance and found work with a competitive poms team and an independent rec team. It was such an amazing experience to pour my passion back into a wonderful group of young ladies and to be in the studio again.

I was working at PayCo from eight to five, then driving down to teach at a dance studio a few nights a week. Through all of it, my heart felt so full. I was finally doing work that I loved. I was finally surrounded by good people that were kind and gentle. Everything felt right.

The only problem was a bit of loneliness. At the time, my mom had ordered two shih tzu online from a breeder, and they were so cute that I couldn't help but want one too. They were purebred, expensive, and way out of my budget, but I fell in love with one just from looking at his picture. His name was Mister, and in the end, my manager bought him for me. When he arrived on an airplane from Oklahoma, I went to the airport to pick him up and absolutely fell in love.

It must be said: he was *so* stinking cute. Everybody loved him. *Everyone* wanted to pet, cuddle, play with, and throw the ball to Mister. Even on Halloween, I'd open the door for the trick-or-treaters, and they'd see Mister and forget all about the candy. He was a difficult puppy and drove me absolutely nuts but became my partner in crime and my ride or die through my twenties and beyond. It was so grounding for me to always have a best friend around, and the responsibility of caring for him always gave me a reason to come home.

At PayCo, I worked with my manager to do whatever was necessary to get a promotion and go into what they called mid- or major-markets sales: selling to companies with more than fifty employees. We laid out a full chart with all the things I'd have to accomplish to get there.

I dealt with quite a bit of adversity clawing my way to the finish line. Nobody went onto the major-markets sales team without the commensurate experience, and I was still young and without a degree, although working hard to earn it. All the new salespeople had to start out on the small-business sales team, which I didn't want to do—I'd been working on the major-markets team as an administrative assistant all along. Though it was unconventional, going straight to major markets just made sense—I knew the team, the product, the lingo, and the ins and outs of the process from being a sales-operations person.

One of my main objectives was getting out into the field with the sales team for experience, and another was to take a couple of Dale Carnegie classes, which PayCo also paid for. Day by day, I was able to level up and get the education I needed. By the time I got into my second year, I was really elevating myself in the company. I earned a number of raises, quit smoking, cleaned up my life, and had matured considerably.

With consistent coaching from my manager, I learned to be more humble, sweet, and kind when dealing with people, but with most of my coworkers, the damage was already done. I couldn't extricate myself from the bad first impression I'd made, and my age and lack of a degree didn't help. To make matters worse, they all knew I was ambitious and gunning for major markets. From day one, they were constantly telling my manager—as well as *his* manager—that I wasn't ready and that promoting me would be the worst decision he'd ever make.

But then, in May 2008, after two years working into the role, I ended up on speakerphone with the regional manager—my manager's manager—who gave me the good news that I'd made it. They sent me up to the company's corporate headquarters in Rochester, New York, for two weeks. If I managed to successfully complete their core training program there, when I came back, I'd finally have a full-time seat on the major-market sales team back home in Denver.

When I arrived, most of what I wound up feeling was fear and impostor syndrome. I was the youngest person in the class, with the least amount of experience, and I still hadn't quite finished my college degree. I felt so underqualified, and it scared me. I couldn't help thinking, *They're going to find me out.* I was terrified that at any moment they'd look at me and say, *You can't be here. You're not good enough.*

I fought through all of that by trying to channel it into being the best in the class, and that's exactly what happened. Soon, my manager back home was getting calls from the people training me saying, "Who is this Mary person? She's quite talented. You made the right move putting her in here. We think she's going to be very, very good." After two weeks of workshops, classes, and a final test, I made the grade, and it was one of the greatest accomplishments of my life. I felt like I had defied the odds and that, after all the hard work, I'd finally found my reward.

Yet when I came back from my corporate training, I was still scared to death, because now I actually had to *do* sales. It was one thing to talk a big game for years while working to earn my spot. Now I finally *had* it, and after two weeks with training wheels, now I actually had to do it and do it well.

The base salary for my position was $42,000 a year. As an administrative assistant, I'd started at $29,000 a year, gotten a few raises, and ended up making around $33,000 a year. I'd effectively earned a $9,000 raise just by taking on a sales role. I was still teaching dance part time, so with the little extra money I had, I went out and bought a bunch of power suits to show up and look the part—I wanted so much to look just like all the veteran women on my team.

So there I was: day one, back in Denver, twenty-four years old, scared to death. While I was sitting there at my desk, fear and anxiety rushed in. For a while, I couldn't even pick up the phone. *What if I mess up?* There was so much riding on my success. I was thinking of the people who had believed in me, and perhaps even more of the people who hadn't, all those who thought it was a joke that my manager had shepherded me into my position.

By this time, he'd been promoted to regional manager, so my other manager, who had also helped me move out of my ex-husband's house, was now my boss. We had a good, long-standing relationship, and I was very excited to be working for him. After staring in terror at the phone on my desk, I had to go into his office for encouragement. *What should I do? I'm panicking. I don't know what I'm doing!*

He just calmly looked at me and said, "Just go and call some of our existing clients. Talk to them. Ask a few basic questions: Why did they choose our service? Why are they still our clients? Even with the competition knocking on their doors, what's the biggest benefit they've gained from *remaining* our clients? Just have friendly conversations and listen to their stories. That should give you the confidence you need to go out and make some real calls. We sell a good product here, and I think you just need to fully believe that. Once you do, you won't be afraid to pick up the phone." I'm so thankful for his wise words—I've told that story over and over, whether in keynotes or pep talks with other salespeople.

I went back to my desk, made some calls, and quickly realized, *Wait. We* do *sell a really great product. I can do this. I* can *be successful.* He was right. Before long, I was feeling fearless. I put my head down, worked crazy hours, and gave the job my all. The first month of company rankings came out for the new fiscal year, and within thirty days, I was on top. In my first month, I became our *number one* rep.

I thought, *This can't be. You've gotta be kidding me. I just started. I'm so young. I don't have any experience. I don't know anything.* Yet, despite everything everyone had said to me, it was true. The feeling of accomplishment I had in those early days was so rewarding, and it made me realize, *Maybe I* am *worth something. Maybe I'm* not *so bad, after all. Maybe I* am *good at something. Maybe sales is just one of those things that comes naturally to me, and I can actually make a great career out of it. I'm going to give this thing everything I have.*

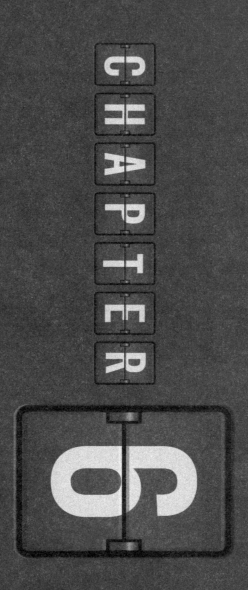

CHAPTER 6

CHAPTER 6

From that moment, I resolved to never sink to number two. I wanted to be number one *forever*, and soon I was grinding to the point of exhaustion. I just hustled and hustled and hustled. My quota was $150,000, which they call a *baby quota* for salespeople in their first year. The top salesperson's performance in my position to date was just over $300,000, so I thought, *Well, that's the number to beat.* By the end of the year, not only had I beat her record, but I'd more than doubled it—I sold $758,000, which was also more than the people in second and third place combined.

I made so much money that year—I'd get commission checks for $10,000 or even $15,000. I had never seen money like that in my *life*, especially in a single check. Unfortunately, that quickly led to the start of some bad behavior. I was still trying to heal from the belief that I wasn't good enough, and it spiraled into an addiction to success. Rather taking that time to *truly* heal, I attacked my internal wounds by seeking recognition, money, and rankings. The satisfaction of those things only lasts for a short moment—it's like a drug, and I was instantly hooked. More and more, I did whatever it took to continue to win, win, win.

Meanwhile, my former manager was entering into a personal season of separation and ultimately divorce. His marriage had already been on the rocks as I was starting my divorce, and all the while, we'd continued to grow closer and closer. Inevitably, our relationship turned romantic. We did our best to keep it quiet at work, but our coworkers always had their suspicions, simply because we were so close.

And during that time in my life, I needed someone so much: a best friend, somebody to be a mentor to me, someone who had lived a few years ahead, someone to really help me understand this white-collar corporate lifestyle that I'd entered but had never been exposed to. I'd just spent four very dark years in sin: drugs, alcohol, partying, and abuse, and the difference was night and day.

He gave me what I needed and more, and for that I felt so indebted and grateful. We had a beautiful, safe relationship, and it lifted me up. He adored and took very good care of me and had so much going for him. He was levelheaded, kind, beloved by many, respected, talented, successful, well dressed, and well traveled; and had a nice car and house; *and* was a good golfer—all the things that the world tells you to do. All the while, he was also a jolly, delightful person.

I continued to excel as a salesperson, but despite all the money and recognition, there were downsides. There's a work-hard, play-hard culture that's pervasive in sales. I increasingly found myself falling into the trap of happy hours and nighttime events. We'd have corporate trainings, and after the work-related activities, groups of us would go out, hit the clubs, and party all night long. The most notorious of these was our annual President's Club trip, which was basically a bunch of good-looking, highly successful salespeople mixed with a lot of alcohol, music, clubs, and dancing. People would misbehave like it was spring break, and unfortunately, I got sucked into that as well.

I'd never felt like I fit in anywhere, at least at this level, and then, all of a sudden, I felt loved, valuable, cared for, and that I *belonged*. As a result, I fell harder and harder into that lifestyle. I was making a lot of money and finally felt successful, and I wanted to make sure everyone around me knew it.

I wanted to be *known*. My ego grew, which threw my priorities out of whack. I let the press go to my head, which made me arrogant and prideful. I became extremely competitive, which turned me into a rotten young woman. The success became a compulsion to the extent that I wasn't afraid to trample over others to reach my objectives. I was addicted, and I would do anything to get another hit. I craved the recognition because, deep down, I was broken and hurt.

> I'd never felt like I fit in anywhere, and then, all of a sudden, I felt loved, valuable, cared for, and that I belonged.

As I continued to make more and more money, guess who came back into my life? In the intervening months, my mom had since lost *her* job. She'd been on state unemployment for twelve months, was about to go on federal unemployment, and had been lying about interviewing for jobs in an effort to extend her unemployment. Now in her fifties, she'd reached a point where she simply no longer cared. When she decided she was no longer going to work, she proceeded to game the system however she could to get the most benefits for the least effort possible.

My parents came to me during this period, apologetic and pulling on my heartstrings. Now that I had the extra income, I again started to help them pay their expenses, mortgage, utility bills, and all the rest.

I felt like I was truly becoming my own woman, and felt a bit safer trying to bring them back into my life as a result. Now that I had a more stable foundation, I felt less that their opinions mattered and, at least to a certain extent, that I'd moved on. Still, I'd never managed to truly stand up to my mom. I'd never told her that she was mean or when she was in the wrong. Instead, I'd always done everything I could to try to make her life better in hope that she would finally love me.

The more I thrived on my own two feet, the more conscious I became of how young I still was. My manager was eighteen years older than me, and sometimes it was hard not to notice. I started to consider that, through my three serious back-to-back relationships, I'd not been single for any significant period of time. I'd met my ex-husband a month after breaking up with my high school sweetheart, and soon after I'd freed myself from him, my friendship with my manager turned romantic.

I started to feel like I'd have regrets if I settled down again. My manager already had three kids and didn't want more, and that caused me to panic a bit—what if I woke up in four years and wanted a baby? I didn't want to go through another breakup at thirty only to try to start a new relationship from scratch. The more I pursued this line of thinking, the more I realized that I wasn't in the right relationship for me.

When I ended it, it was devastating. I had so much love and respect for him. He had saved me in so many ways. He'd offered me a job when he probably shouldn't have. He invested in me as a human, as a person, and as a friend. He mentored me, guided me through an impressionable time in my life, and took very good care of me. He never harmed or hurt me, never said anything mean, and was so loving and patient, and I'm still forever grateful for what he did for me throughout that beautiful chapter of my life. I am very sorry for the way that I ended it—I hurt him, and he didn't deserve it.

For a while, we were still working together at PayCo, and before long it became unbearable. I couldn't even be in the same room with him. To make matters worse, we'd both used the same real estate agent to purchase condos in the same neighborhood, just a few streets apart, and were using the same general contractor to refurbish them. Soon after I realized I couldn't be in the same room as him at work, I realized that I couldn't be in the same neighborhood either. I'd run into him constantly—at the gym, at the pool, at the bar, at the clubhouse.

Before long I went back to our real estate agent for a reprieve, and she helped me find a fully furnished two-story loft in downtown Denver, where I could breathe a little easier. By the time I rented out my condo and moved across town, I was twenty-eight, with two homes and two cars. I'd paid cash for a BMW Z4 roadster convertible—a superflashy little sports car that drove like a go-kart on the highway. It was small, dangerous, and a little scary to drive, but I absolutely loved it.

Despite all the trappings of success, I missed my ex terribly and started hating my life without him. For a while, I was lost. When our next President's Club trip rolled around, I went to Miami and caught a virus that was going around. Beyond giving me mono-like symptoms, it aggressively attacked my liver. When the doctors measured the marker enzyme in my liver, it was elevated out of proportion. I pushed through as far as managing my energy, but it wasn't easy.

I was still drinking more and more and going out entirely too much. I could feel myself sliding into a bad downward spiral and knew I was starting to lose control. I'd been our number one rep for two years, but my numbers were starting to slip. I wasn't taking care of myself, and as a result, I wasn't performing. As everything piled up,

I decided to take a leave of absence from work—catching that virus gave me an ironclad reason, as I was clearly not physically well enough to work, but I left just as much to get over my ex.

Without a doubt, I needed the time off. I started to rest, went on therapies for my liver, and cut back on drinking and going out. I also started to make some important decisions about what I wanted to do with my life. It was obvious that I couldn't stay at that company as long as my ex was there. Whenever I'd need to talk to him about something, I wanted to just jump across the desk and throw myself at him, just to embrace him and be comforted.

As I started feeling better, I began using my suddenly ample free time to focus more on dance. My body had fully healed after my accident, so I got back into hip-hop and break dancing. I joined a crew in Denver called Motion 303 and jumped right back in to dancing professionally. I fell into a relationship with a man named Jeremy, a much younger dancer on the crew, and we decided to go in on a big six-bedroom house with six roommates near the University of Denver. He was a wonderful person but young and rudderless, and he and my new roommates sucked me right back into partying.

I considered my next chapter for work, and the first thing that came to mind was one of my clients, a start-up called Grow LLC, which handled bookkeeping, accounting, payroll, and HR for small businesses. I'd already known them for some time, and really enjoyed working with their management team. After I planted a seed with them, they told me they could use a head of sales and marketing to help grow the company. I did a couple of casual interviews, sat in on some of their board meetings, and got an idea of where their financials were. As soon as I had the job secured, I resigned from PayCo—I never returned from my leave of absence.

It had been fun to take a three-month leave, transform from a corporate salesperson into a professional dancer, and date someone new, but now I knew it was time to wise up, get back in the game, and do something with my life. I broke up with Jeremy, moved back into my condo in Highlands Ranch, and traded my Xterra and Z4 for a BMW 328i—still a convertible, but at least one that was mostly usable year round.

With all of that handled, I officially signed on with Grow as their new vice president of sales and marketing, and that became one of the most remarkable experiences of my life. I'd never done anything at that level. I'd also never worked for a start-up.

> **I read a couple of books on marketing, leveraged what I'd learned from studying for my degree, and went for it.**

Their founder was working for equity and not taking a paycheck. They were in the start-up phase and only making $120,000 a year in annual revenue. I took an equity position myself, which brought my income down to $3,000 a month. They asked how much money I needed to survive, and that's the number I gave them—even after giving so much to my parents, my savings were still decent.

It felt very much like the start of a new chapter: huge title, young lady, not a lot of leadership or marketing experience. But by this point, I'd been in a similar position before, and I just decided to own it. I read a couple of books on marketing, leveraged what I'd learned from studying for my degree, and went for it. Working with a small executive team involved a lot of ego and friction, but together we were able to quadruple the size of that company in seven months, which brought our annual revenue to roughly $480,000.

In the process, I had the time of my life. I learned what I could do beyond sales: go-to-market strategy, brand strategy, developing marketing and sales enablement collateral, brochure design, building a sales team, recruiting and onboarding people, and more. Plus, I was only twenty-seven—to have the opportunity to do all of that at my age was remarkable.

Working for Grow was also the first time I'd dealt with any sort of sexism at the office. I was highly respected by the time I left PayCo, where most of the top salespeople were women. The CFO at Grow and I had a brother-sister, love-hate relationship. I'd be sitting at my cubicle trying to work, and he'd burst out of his office to throw squishy balls at me. He was immature, to say the least.

At Grow, I'd do a design for new marketing campaign, and he'd send it back covered in red ink, tell me it was horrible, and tell me to go back to the drawing board to come up with a new idea. Then, at the team meeting the next day, he'd present my original idea—the one he'd redlined and said was terrible—as his own, and I'd have to sit there and listen to everyone telling him how amazing it and he was.

It was all so brazen that at first I had no idea how to react. Despite my growth and success at PayCo, I still didn't know how to speak up for myself. Eventually, we started to butt heads. I got sick of the immature way he approached our relationship, and could never truly get a read on him.

Aside from that, I really enjoyed working there. To this day I retain a lot of respect for the owner, who was older, calm, and kind, and had become a great friend to me. I'd also accumulated more skills at PayCo and while getting my degree than I gave myself credit for. I'd created a lot of my own one-pagers and marketing mailers to send out as part of my top-of-funnel prospecting and did my own email copy and outbound emails. We didn't have automation then, like we do now, so I'd been sending every email manually. I also developed and hosted HR events and webinars and, in so doing, got to invite subject matter experts and thought leaders to contribute. I was an early adopter of LinkedIn and used it heavily for top-of-funnel prospecting, connections, creating posts, and marketing in general. At Grow, I surprised even myself, pulling all kinds of tricks out of my hat in a completely new context.

Around that time, I was introduced to a lady named Helen through one of the CFOs I'd worked with at PayCo. I knew I wanted to start my own company, but I hadn't yet put all the pieces together. I'd scaled a professional services company, but I didn't yet have experience in tech or software as a service (SaaS). I wanted to work for Helen as an employee for a few months, mostly to learn, and learn I did. After only a few months, I was starting to feel like I knew a thing or two about internet and tech start-ups, go-to-market, and business strategy.

She was running an online search directory start-up, and in working with her, I got to build out a sales team and help take them to market. It was my first time working with a technology start-up, and I loved it. I began going to networking events to bring on more clients, and the whole thing took off. I found it amazing that all these start-ups and entrepreneurs were willing to work with me—I was still very young and figuring it out as I went.

I loved business-strategy work, and more and more, I wanted to do it full time. So, at the ripe old age of twenty-eight, I started my first company as a go-to-market and business strategist. I named it Butterfly Creative—I've always loved the symbol of a creature that starts as a caterpillar, goes into a cocoon, and emerges as a beautiful butterfly. My mission was to help start-ups, entrepreneurs, and founders take their rough visions and turn them into viable business plans. I took what I knew, packaged it into a bundle of service offerings, and launched it into the market.

I moved from an employee to a contractor for Helen, and she let me have part of her office space to run my company. Especially after some of my experiences at Grow, it was great to work with a female founder. She was a total lady boss, and I had a lot of respect for her. She knew how to command a room filled with executives and investors, had a great vision, introduced me to all kinds of people, and generally took great care of me. She really knew how to play the game of power and money, got audiences with who's-who kinds of people, and used every ounce of her beauty, influence, and intelligence to make it all happen.

But as glamorous as all this may sound, I was still struggling. I missed my ex-boyfriend every day, and I started drinking more and more. I was out partying every night. There were a lot of sales, networking, and other events to attend during the day, and at night I'd come home and crank out all the related deliverables. I'd often find myself sitting there, working and going through a bottle of wine. I'd fill my glass back up over and over, sometimes opening yet another bottle, and drinking and working until I passed out.

Right as I had been getting myself on the right track, I met a guy at the bar—yet another awful alcoholic who made me feel like a pile of crap. He had the exact same tendencies as my ex-husband: he was highly controlling, played mind games, gave me the cold shoulder, avoided eye contact, and stopped talking to me for no reason—the works. I wouldn't even know what I'd done to upset him, and he'd just start giving me the silent treatment. He was also a smoker, so I fell back into that bad habit again. He was not a good influence at all— we'd go up to the clubhouse in my neighborhood to drink and party every night. But I *was* learning, albeit slowly—I managed to end it after a few months, as the relationship clearly wasn't serving me at all.

I then agreed to meet with a former PayCo CFO client named Paul, who I started dating next. He looked like Bradley Cooper, and was so buttoned up, classy, and conservative—ultimately a bit *too* conservative for me. He was so sweet and very professional, and I was still a little rough around the edges, trying to grow out of being a party girl.

When that ended, I went hard on dating apps and Match.com. I was relentless. I had a full-on pipeline going and couldn't go a week without a new first date. I simply could not function without a date lined up on the calendar. I never took the time to just be independent, single, and alone with my thoughts. Every night I'd find myself sitting there, drinking martinis, eating Cheetos, and swiping on dating apps, having conversations with a bunch of strangers. Like so many women, I could write a book on bad dating stories. I had many awful first dates: men who didn't look like their pictures, men who lied and fabricated, and men whose only agenda was hooking up, which was not what I was looking for.

While dating apps gave me the opportunity to meet many different types of people, I found that, unfortunately, most guys out there made me even sadder. One after the other, they made me miss my ex—he was really the cream of the crop, the best of the best. Every time I went on another terrible date, I realized even more how big a mistake I'd made in breaking up with him, and the more I dated, the more miserable it made me. I just could not find the one, or anyone even close.

Worse, I was still failing to take the time to heal and figure out what was wrong with *me*. I masked what was really going on, chasing the shiny accoutrements of success, all of which the world told me I should want. All the while, I was buying into the empty promise that those things would make my life worth living.

Then, one day at a networking event, I met a chiropractor named Leif. When we hit it off, it felt different. We were both young, hungry, ambitious, aspiring entrepreneurs, and it was fun dating him. He adored me and was kind. We were still a little reckless with all our drinking and partying, but we also knew how to get down to business and just crank. There was so much of that going on that for a while, things stayed casual—at least at first.

Starting my own business meant that I didn't have a direct manager or teammates, and with no one holding me accountable, partying and alcohol took over my life, and it increasingly became a struggle to control my days. As I made my own hours, the bottles of wine started coming out earlier and earlier. I started pushing aside work to go out and party instead, especially on the weekends.

With no one holding me accountable, partying and alcohol took over my life.

I lived in a gated community with its own bar and restaurant attached to a big outdoor resort-style pool. On the weekends, I'd go there and start drinking as soon as they opened at eleven in the morning, hang out all day, go home and pass out around four o'clock, and sleep it off for a couple of hours. Then I'd wake up intoxicated, shower, get myself together, change into party clothes, and go right back for live music or karaoke. I'd dance until two in the morning, go home hammered, sleep off the hangover, rinse, and repeat. It was a very scary way to live.

During the day, in my quasi-sober hours, I was still somehow running a pretty darn successful business. I still had plenty to learn: I was young and took on too much, and didn't yet know how to price my services, say no, or delegate. And more than anything, I didn't know how to manage the alcoholism that was gradually taking over my life. But God has a funny way of getting our attention.

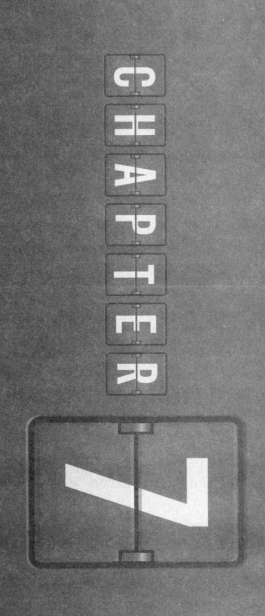

CHAPTER 7

CHAPTER 7

One fateful Memorial Day weekend, I had plans to meet a friend, go boating, and stay at a campground in her family's RV. I love boating—I refuse to get in the water because I'm afraid of having an unwanted interaction with the various things swimming in it, but I definitely love sitting on a boat, getting a nice dark tan, drinking Coronas, smoking cigarettes, and generally having a great time.

I also had plans to go see my grandmother, Mary, whom I loved more than anything, on the way there. She was a bright, beautiful, kind, gentle, calm, centered woman who saw so much beauty in this world. She didn't have the fiery passion that I do, but she was so wise and always had the answer to everything. She knew about the challenges that my parents had and was always a very safe place for my brother and me. I just loved being with her. Plus, she was godly! She was the only person in my family that had a strong faith, regularly attended the Greek Orthodox church, and was passionate about her attendance there. Aside from being named after her, I look like her, which I love.

By that time, she'd aged into her nineties and could no longer live on her own. My parents offered for her to move in with them, which she did for a couple of years. As her health declined further, she made the decision to move out of their house and into assisted living. She couldn't go up and down the stairs and was starting to lose control of her bladder, which was embarrassing for her. She was wicked smart and sharp till the day she died, so it was hard for her to be trapped in an aging body. Not long after going into assisted living, she went into hospice, and that's where she was that Memorial Day weekend, so I'd made plans to go see her on Saturday morning before heading to the campground to see my friends.

The night before I left, I thought, *Hey, it's Friday night, and I've worked really hard this week. I'm cutting out early. It's Memorial Day weekend, so I'm gonna party.* I drove my BMW convertible over to the clubhouse in my neighborhood, which was unusual—most of the time, I just walked over, but I really loved showing off that convertible. I hadn't yet met Jesus and was being raised and run by this world, which continually reinforces that you're important if you make money and have a nice car. I still wanted to feel important, and I wanted people to like me. I always made sure to play the music really loud, thinking it would make people think, *Wow, look at her. Isn't she great?* It was a sad way to live, but unfortunately, that's who I was at twenty-eight.

My plan was to tie one on and party hard, and that's exactly what I did. I drank one vodka soda with cranberry after the other, sang karaoke, and danced to the music until I was drunk enough to pass out. Then I got into my car, headed home, and made a left turn directly into my neighbors' front porch.

Thankfully, they were not home. I hit my head hard enough to break the rearview mirror off its mount. I had a concussion and nasty contusions on my face, and I again realized that my life was about to change, because I was about to get in a lot of trouble. It had been ten years, one month, and one day since my last accident.

I didn't know what to do. I tried reversing my car, but my tires were stuck on the brick retaining wall that I'd just demolished. I couldn't back up or hide the evidence of what I'd done. I was only thirty feet from my house, so I decided to just leave the car there and walk back home. I knew the police would be called, but I was drunk, and I didn't have a lot of sense in the moment.

I went back into my house to let my dog out, then made a phone call to my friend Brice. *Hey, I crashed my car, and the police are probably going to be here any moment. I've been drinking, am probably going to jail, and I don't know how long I'm going to be gone. Could you come pick up my dog?*

My friend came by, and so did the police. After I admitted to crashing the car, they did a sobriety test right in front of my house. I knew a bit about sentencing for people in my shoes, so I declined the Breathalyzer in favor of a blood test. They took me to the hospital, where I clocked in at 0.219, well over the legal driving limit of 0.08 and enough to get a more serious sentence.

I was booked and went to jail. I've been through some low moments in my life, but getting booked felt like the lowest of all. I was coming off the best run of my entire life. The opportunity to work at PayCo had saved me. I'd escaped the toxic, scary life I'd been living, but because I didn't know how to handle my new life with care, I'd let it consume me. The success, money, and recognition became an addiction. I partied too hard, and now I knew without a doubt that I'd lost control of my life.

What do you do at that point? I'd never been caught breaking the law, except for when we'd violated the curfew as teenagers. Getting "arrested" at sixteen is different—they take you to juvie, which looks like a community center, then tell you what to do and help you call your parents. Real jail, of course, is no walk in the park. I had no idea what the process was, how to get out, the extent of my injuries, or what laws I'd broken. For all I knew, they could have held me for months.

When I was in jail, the first person I thought about was my grandma. She was dying, and I was supposed to go and see her, and I was sure she would wonder why I wasn't there. The next time I saw her, she was sleeping peacefully, and the time after that, I showed up twenty minutes too late.

Next, I thought of my friends waiting for me at the campground. Then my mind went to my clients. What are they going to think? Would I lose them? The shame and the guilt were by far the worst part. I started blaming myself for screwing up everything good in my life.

I was also afraid I was going to turn out just like my mom. Then, of course, the only people I could think to call were my parents. I wanted to avoid that if possible, so in my state I thought it'd be a bright idea to call my sister, who was still living in Indiana. I didn't know that when you call from jail, the operator announces to the other line that you're making a collect call from county jail. When I called her house in the middle of the night, one of her kids answered the phone and hung right up.

At that point, I didn't know who to call or what to do. I had just bashed my head and was still drunk and emotionally unwell. I couldn't pull myself together enough to think of what to do next, so I decided to sleep it off and deal with it in the morning. When I woke up, the police explained the process of getting bonded out. At that time, the only people whose phone numbers I knew by heart were my parents.

Let me tell you how not great calling *them* felt. It was like saying, *Hey, you guys were right. I* am *a nobody. I* am *a failure, just like you told me for my entire life. I'm sorry for fooling myself and thinking I was worth anything. You were right after all.* Even though I'd been swimming upstream and away from them for my entire life, I had never stopped trying to prove that I was worthy of their love and recognition.

They came and bailed me out— of course, with my money—and then drove me home. It was a short ride, no more than twenty minutes. For the entirety of the drive, they told me exactly what I'd anticipated: that I was

> **I had never stopped trying to prove that I was worthy of their love and recognition.**

a failure, that I had thrown my life away, that this was the biggest mistake I could have ever made, that I would never rebound, that my life as a professional was over as I knew it, that I'd never be employed again, and that no one would want to do business with me after this entered the public record. Then, they dropped me off at my house.

I texted Brice, and when he arrived, he didn't say two words to me, and when he left, he just shook his head. I was reeling from my concussion, and my head was pounding. No amount of Tylenol could take the pain away. I laid my head on my pillow that night and just wanted to die. In my mind, I had lost everything and was no good to anyone, including myself.

Though I didn't know God back then, I almost found myself praying. I could think of nothing else but the desire to die. I could not imagine waking up the next day to face the world and the consequences of what I'd done. The guilt and the shame completely took me over. When I finally fell asleep, the crash and the ride home with my parents played back as nightmares on continuous loop.

The next day, I called another friend who lived in my neighborhood. He came by, gave me a hug, and told me he was going to help me through this and that it was going to be okay. Then we got all the alcohol out of my house. When I started to detox, I did not realize how much of an alcoholic I had become. By this point, my drinking habit had ballooned to either two bottles of wine or three or four martinis per night—in either case, a lot of alcohol for a little body.

For the four or so days it took to detox and start to heal from the concussion, I just sat in the dark. I didn't talk to anyone and just sat there with the shakes. I tried to sleep as much as I could, but that inevitably brought back the recurring nightmares. I was too depressed to even go outside, and besides, the sunlight hurt my eyes and head.

I knew that I had to do something different with my life, and more and more, I realized that I wasn't okay and needed help. One of the blessings of getting a DUI is that therapy afterward is mandatory, and I enrolled as quickly as I could. I started in June and am so grateful for the kind lady that was our group teacher. I don't remember her name, but she had very compassionate eyes. I can remember so vividly how motherly she felt to me. Even though I was in a room with ten other people, I felt like I was the only student in her class.

Through therapy, I finally started understanding the disease of alcoholism and its role in codependency and toxic relationships.

Through therapy, I finally started understanding the disease of alcoholism and its role in codependency and toxic relationships. Very slowly, I started the process of learning to forgive myself. Although it took a long time, things gradually started to make sense. I reassessed how I was living my life and gained a new insight into how and why the cycle I was born into is so destructive. I began to make sense of how, on one hand, I had so many good things going for me, and on the other, I couldn't escape my demons.

After I had paid thousands of dollars in fines, they gave me two hundred hours of community service and two weeks of house arrest, with an ankle monitor and everything. After that, I was on probation for a year, which meant submitting to urine tests at random. Every single morning I'd have to call in to see if my number was selected, and if it had been, I'd have to drive in and do yet another urine test.

They also installed a Breathalyzer in my car, which restricted the car from starting until after I breathed into it to prove that I hadn't been drinking. It was so embarrassing to be reminded of my mistake all day, every day, and I hid it as much as I could from everyone around me. The Breathalyzer would beep when I was driving, and I'd always duck down to inconspicuously blow into it. From then on, I always drove myself everywhere and never let anyone into my car.

I made a commitment to adopt a life of sobriety and to thoroughly clean up my life. As I went through that summer of classes and therapy, I decided to get very serious as a business owner. I resolved to build something that would allow me to do truly good work *and* make good money. As all of this was going on, I was approached by a video producer who had connections with all the local TV stations. He told me he loved what I was doing as an entrepreneur and asked if I'd ever thought about adapting my material for children. I hadn't, but it sounded like a great idea.

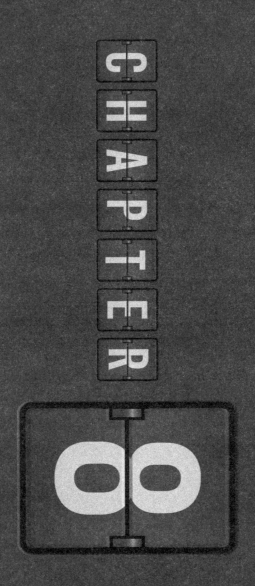

CHAPTER 8

CHAPTER 8

As I started to take my business to the next level, I self-published a book outlining the methodology I used with all my clients—I called it *Extreme Business Building: From Concept to Profit in 60 Days*. It's a short read and full of typos, but I still loved it. I was so proud to be a self-published author, and it gave me a lot of credibility in the circles that I was in. The more serious I became about my work, the more my business thrived.

After talking to that video producer, I started out by adapting my book for youth and running business workshops for both kids and adults. It quickly took off. I rediscovered my passion while working with kids, and it felt so good to use my performing arts talents for the first time in years. I created TV and radio shows; went into a recording studio to produce a full CD; and found myself fully back into acting, singing, and dancing.

After driving my car into my neighbor's front porch, I didn't think I could ever really live it down. I was so embarrassed that I sold my condo and found a job in Fort Morgan, a farm town in the eastern plains of Colorado, teaching dance part time at a school for performing arts. After getting away from where and how I'd been living, I still frequently went back into Denver and crashed on friends' couches while working on other projects.

After my accident, Leif was one of the first people I called—he'd had a DUI himself and had fully gone through the process. He came back into my life at the perfect time—I needed all the help I could get to recover from the accident. I still trusted him, and this time around, our relationship became more serious.

During that time, I met a very special young lady named Rylie while teaching at the dance studio. She was thirteen when I met her, and she was interested in being a part of Million Dollar Butterflies. She soon turned into an entrepreneur and an actress right before my eyes.

I took a great liking to her, and to this day I think she's one of the most remarkable, talented young women I've ever met. At thirteen, she launched her own business, Dance to the Pointe, a clothing brand, a blog, and a vlog. She was more put together as a teen than most adults I've met. She was a shining star on the show, then

My business consulting practice was going well, but getting the show off the ground cost *a lot*.

became my cohost on the radio show, and we always worked extremely well together.

As all this was going on, something troubling was happening beneath the surface: my priorities were still out of order. I was excited about the show *because I wanted to see myself on TV*. I was still so broken and unhealed, and I *still* didn't believe I was worth anything. Especially after the accident and dealing the DUI, I heavily doubted myself. Deep down, I believed that if I could just see myself on TV, then I'd *be someone*. Something turned over in my brain: *If this is what it's gonna take, I'm gonna go all in.*

Unfortunately, going all in became very, very expensive. My business consulting practice was going well, but getting the show off the ground cost a *lot*. I used all my consulting profits to finance it, then ended up cashing in my 401(k) and *then* selling my house, all in the name of keeping the show afloat.

Then I got a text from my brother saying that my aunt had passed away. Auntie Gayle was my mom's sister, and just as bad an alcoholic, if not worse. Her husband had passed away a few years prior, and ever since, she'd lived by herself and drunk all day. In the end, she'd slipped, fell, hit her head, and bled to death. I still don't know how she was found.

My mom had been very close with her, and they'd talked every day. My aunt had two dogs and a whole house of things to take care of, so my mom swiftly arranged a trip back to Indiana to take care of her estate—she acted fast because she knew the formal assessor for the estate wouldn't be far behind.

After months without contact with my family, my grandma, my mom, and my sister Lisa all went back to Indiana together, and it was utter insanity, particularly with my grandmother. At that point she'd just turned eighty, but was still wearing her pink suits, pantyhose, high heels, and pearls, judging everyone and everything in sight. She was as close as I've seen to the evil stepmother in *Cinderella*: mean, critical, proper, superior, righteous, and absolutely ruthless.

At first I thought, *I'm older now. Maybe I can actually talk to her, adult to adult. Maybe we can have an actual conversation.* No, she wanted nothing to do with me. She was still mad at me for my wedding, still harping on how I hadn't made plans for the out-of-town guests. She was doubly disgusted that I'd then gotten a divorce and then triply distraught that she'd heard about it from my parents and not from me personally.

It wasn't long after we arrived that my mom gathered up everything of value at my aunt's, stuffed it into my deceased uncle's truck, bundled up the dogs, and drove everything back to Colorado. Her ultimate plan had been to get as much out before the assessor showed up to execute the will.

For me, it was all too much. Before my other grandma, my yiayia, had gone into hospice, when she was living in my parents' basement, she'd moved her most important heirlooms there from Indiana—furniture, jewelry, and everything else of value. She'd already given me her wedding rings and had promised me that she'd leave me all her jewelry too.

This was during the season that my mom had exhausted state unemployment and was trying to get on extended federal unemployment, as my dad wasn't working either. As soon as my grandma moved into hospice, they knew she wasn't coming back, and they immediately descended to selling off her belongings. They didn't even wait until she died.

My grandma Mary's final wish was to be buried in a plot next to her husband in Indiana, and the plan was for her to be flown back for that to happen. That certainly wouldn't have been cheap, but she had a life insurance policy—nothing massive, but enough to cover the expenses to pay for a proper burial. Instead, as soon as she passed, my parents cremated her for $300 and pocketed the rest of the money. My grandmother was so incredible, and it just felt so awful and mean to take advantage of her and not honor her wishes, and I told my parents how I felt. I was very upset with how they'd handled it, and it became the first time I ever stood up to my mom.

I can't remember the details, because at the time I was still recovering the full function of my memory after my concussion. All I know is that when I finally told my mom how disappointed I was, it was the end of the conversation. Soon thereafter, I received an email from my dad saying how much I'd upset her, and he recommended that we take time apart and not communicate. After seeing my mom looting her recently deceased family members twice, I wanted nothing more to do with her and cut off communication all over again.

It was months before I received a random text message from them with an invitation to Thanksgiving. I still wasn't on speaking terms with my mom, so my first thought was, *Are you kidding me? Why?* Then, I don't know why, but my next thought was, *What the heck? I'll give it a try.*

Then, when I showed up, no one spoke to me. No one asked any questions or directed conversation toward me. For the entire evening, it was as if I were invisible—it was the most awkward, *Twilight Zone* experience of my life. I still don't know why they'd invited me in the first place.

I remember getting in the car and just breaking down afterward—I couldn't even believe what had happened. By that point, I'd been through some weird things with my family, and this topped them all. I still don't remember a lot of the details due to my head trauma, and I think I've buried a lot of the rest.

The very next day, my parents texted saying that they'd love to have me over for Christmas. To this day, I don't know whether the whole thing was one big sick mind game.

Meanwhile, I was also becoming frustrated with Leif. If he wasn't quite a fully fledged, card-carrying alcoholic, he still certainly spent a lot of time binge drinking. More and more, his stories seemed inconsistent, and he'd often break plans for reasons that weren't entirely clear.

All of this came to a head on Christmas Eve. He eventually passed out drunk, and as he snored on the couch, I was left to take care of his daughter. After I got her to bed, I felt that something seemed sufficiently off, and I couldn't help but go through his phone. There, I immediately found text message threads with multiple women, and they went back for *months*. I was clearly far from the only woman in his life, and I instantly knew it was the end. I was just so tired of all the toxic relationships, the drama, and the abuse, in all its forms.

He left that night, but he was supposed to come back the next morning. Later that night, he sent me a text saying he wouldn't be coming back the next day after all—he wanted to stay at his baby-mama-ex-girlfriend's for the sake of their daughter, so she could wake up with both of her parents on Christmas morning. Had I not known the truth, I probably would have been accommodating as usual. Now I knew they were still involved and that I wasn't being put first, which only broke my heart further.

I looked around, thinking, *This is not what I was created for.*

I woke up on Christmas alone. I had no family, and now I had no boyfriend. A month prior, I'd moved back to a small smelly low-income-housing apartment in Highlands Ranch. It was across the street from another dance studio I was teaching at, and it was all I could afford.

I looked around, thinking, *This is not what I was created for.* I felt like I was throwing my life away. I was poor from shoveling all my savings and equity into getting Million Dollar Butterflies off the ground, and in doing so, I had thoroughly exhausted myself. I knew beyond a doubt that something needed to change in my life.

In some kind of trance, I went to a Village Inn diner—it was the only place I could think of that would be open Christmas morning. I sat down in a booth, makeup-less and in a winter hat, and just started crying. I could not pull myself together. I knew I had to change, because I couldn't go another day carrying so much heartache.

Eventually, I was moved to text my friend, an ex-pastor. I asked if he was at home, and when he said yes, I nonchalantly headed straight to his apartment. It was freezing that day—it couldn't have been more than maybe six or seven degrees Fahrenheit. When I got there, I sat outside his apartment door in the elements, freezing, continuing to text him as if I wasn't right outside: "What are your plans for Christmas? What are you doing today?"

After going back and forth for a while, I think he could sense that something was up and just asked point-blank what I needed. At that point, I broke down and said I'd been outside his door all along. When he opened it, I just lost it. I was hysterical. I couldn't even stand up, so I scooted my way inside and just sat on his floor, bawling.

At first, he couldn't believe what he was seeing. "What's going on? What do you need?"

All I could muster was that I couldn't continue living this way. There *had* to be something greater. I expressed how disappointed I was in life—I'd done everything the world had told me to do but still felt like a failure, broken and empty inside. I told him how confusing it was to feel so unfulfilled—despite the money, awards, recognition, and accolades. I was supposed to be smart, filled with potential, and have all kinds of unique skills and talents. My situation didn't make sense, and it felt like it was crushing me. I just cried my heart out to him, and finally said it again: *There has to be something more to life than this.*

At that point, he looked at me and said, "There is." Then he opened his Bible. He started from the very first page in Genesis, and read to me. Suddenly, for the first time, I had ears to hear, and my heart opened. God had been pursuing me for years, and I was finally ready to listen and accept his invitation. My friend read to me for quite some time, spoke life over me, and prayed for me.

Eventually, I calmed down. At the time, I didn't know anything about God, Jesus, or the Bible. I grew up going to Greek Orthodox church, but the services were literally *in Greek*, and I didn't understand a word. I'd gone to Sunday school, too, but there we'd just sat and read an old-school Bible line by line. I was a seven-year-old girl—on top of not being able to distinguish *ye* from *thee*, my Sunday school teachers were all Greek and had thick accents. I mostly just liked going to church for the cookies and lemonade.

My friend asked if I had a church I could go to, or any friends who could bring me to one. I told him that my friend Vicki had been attending a church called Journey near my apartment, and I texted her to ask if she'd bring me. She replied right away: "Of course."

I took my friend's Bible home with me that day and just kept reading and reading. When the next service rolled around, Vicki brought me along, and the whole experience was unbelievable— I couldn't believe the words on the screen as everyone was singing worship. It was all about love, and I just didn't get it. I was utterly confused by their idea, or their definition, of love. As they sang about God's love for his people, and how his people love and worship him in return, I simply could neither understand nor believe it. I'd just never seen love practiced like that. At first, I didn't think it was real, but I went back to church with my friend week after week and kept dutifully reading my Bible.

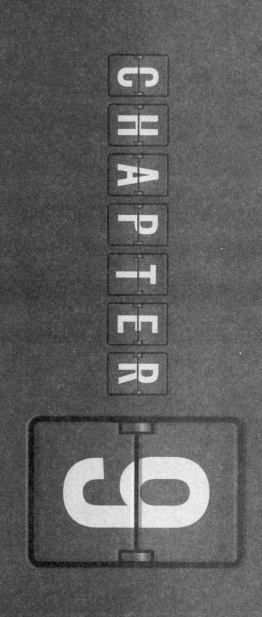

CHAPTER 9

CHAPTER 9

n late January, a friend at the radio station told me I should meet her friends Sarah and Rebecca. "They run a women's ministry called She Shares, and they also have a radio show. Maybe that's something you could tap into." I went and met them both, and another woman named Angie came along. She'd been a news reporter on channel 2 in Denver for years—I'd always loved seeing her on TV and thought she was incredible. She'd left the news to start a radio show at my same station, and it was a bit surreal to be introduced to her.

One fateful night soon thereafter, all three ladies invited me to an event for their group, but I did *not* feel like going. I'd been working so hard on building up Million Dollar Butterflies and was out of energy. I'd worked since the moment I'd woken that morning and had finally taken a break to shower. I'd planned on working for the rest of the night and was in no mood to go out into the world. Yet Angie just kept texting me and texting me, telling me I needed to get out of the house. Finally, I gave in. *Okay, fine.*

I met her at the event and immediately met many amazing women. I listened to some of their stories and witnessed everyone praying for one another. I found the whole scene empowering, and even shared a little bit of my own story, but was still a bit shy and reserved.

By the end of the night, Sarah and I had hit it off, and we made plans to get coffee. When we eventually went, she asked about my dating life. Right away I told her, *Dude, I'm never dating ever again.* After Leif, I'd entirely written it off. I wanted to focus on my business to get it on track and profitable, because I was rapidly running out of money. To this she said, "Well, I'm pretty well connected, so if I can help you in either area, let me know."

By mid-February, another event rolled around. This time it was a chocolate, wine, and hot-tub night. I was still sober, so I skipped the wine, but I was more than happy to hang out and eat chocolate in a hot tub. As we were sitting in the water, Sarah started prodding me about dating again.

"Who's your perfect guy?"

I had to think for a second. "Okay: midthirties, handsome—but not *GQ* handsome, where he's a player and obsessed with himself and always at the gym. Just a normal, good-looking guy. Conservative, never married, no kids, good job, stable, has a house, sweet, works hard, takes care of people, and comes from a great family."

As I finished listing off everything I could think of, I laughed, went for more chocolate, chuckled, and added, "And he doesn't exist."

Then Sarah looked dead at me and said, "He *does* exist, and his name is David."

She dried off her hands and grabbed her phone.

"I'm going to show you his picture. He lives in Parker. He's thirty-five, single, never married, no kids, has had the same job for fifteen years, and comes from the best family ever. They're so sweet. He's a Christian, and he's conservative, *and* everything else."

I rolled my eyes. "If he really was all those things, then he wouldn't be single."

"No. He *is*. He just got out of a bad breakup. He was single for most of his twenties, then got into a relationship with some girl who just trampled all over him and broke his heart. He is not really someone to just go out on dates, so he's been single ever since. I don't think he ever wants to date again either. So you're in the same place."

Meanwhile, I was looking at his pictures, and he was so handsome. I was reluctant to admit it, but I was thinking, *Oh, my gosh. You've got to be kidding me. This is too good to be true.*

Then she looked at me and said, "Let's see if he's interested in meeting you."

Lo and behold, he texted her right back and said he *was* interested in meeting me. He was up in the mountains in Breckenridge with his family at that time, but we set a date for Sarah, her husband, and the two of us to go out together on the ninth of March.

Leading up to it, I have to admit: I was excited. Though we never spoke on the phone, we did send a couple of messages back and forth on Facebook. We were messaging as Rylie and I headed to a high school musical to see Meg, one of the other kids from Million Dollar Butterflies, perform. As we were sitting in our seats waiting for the show to start, I got another message from David saying he was excited to meet, and I had no idea what to say back. I turned to Rylie, this seasoned girl of thirteen, and sought her dating advice.

She shrugged and told me to send him some emojis.

At that point I had to ask, "What's an emoji?" Forgive me; it was 2013. Rylie proceeded to help me install emojis on my keyboard so I could send my very first to David. Something about this felt different. I felt like *I* was sixteen and going on *my* first date.

Then, it started to get really cold. As the Denver weather people overdramatized the forecasts as usual, it got me thinking and making any excuse I could. "There's a blizzard coming in. I probably won't be able to make the date. It's going to be cold. Plus, I'm so busy with work."

Two days before the date, they were still predicting a blizzard, a massive freeze, and temperatures solidly in the negative. Right as I was about to cancel, I thought, *Let's wait and see how I feel in the morning.*

Then, that night, I had the most vivid dream I've ever had. In the dream, David appeared to me in full form. I'd never heard his voice, but he spoke to me. I dreamed we had our first date, and then many more dates, and fell in love. We got married, had a baby, and lived a whole lifetime together. When I woke up, I thought, *If my life can even be a fraction of that dream, then I'm going on this date.*

When David came into the house, I about fell over. He looked exactly like he had in the dream.

Without fail, it got *so* cold, and that huge snowstorm came in. Yet no one canceled. We all met at Josh and Sarah's house. The plan was to go to church together, then get something to eat.

When David came into the house, I about fell over. He looked exactly like he had in the dream. When he opened his mouth to say hello, I knew it was *him*. He has a unique voice, and it sounded *exactly* like the one I heard in my dream. I knew he was a gift from God.

I was in such a state of disbelief that I couldn't compose myself. I ducked around the table and pretended that I had something stuck in my eye to avoid having to shake his hand. After I finally pulled myself together, we at least managed to sit down for a few minutes and talk. We all proceeded to church, enjoyed the worship and the sermon, had dinner at a restaurant called John Holly's, then went back to Josh and Sarah's house.

Josh is an aspiring entrepreneur and was excited about Million Dollar Butterflies. He had all kinds of business-building questions for me. After David took in our conversation, he turned to me and said, "Wow, you really do a *lot*." I think it was all a little surprising to him—he'd never met anyone like me, and I think it was intriguing for him to meet someone with so much going on.

We knew at the end of that night that we wanted to see each other again. I can boldly tell you it was love at first sight, and that I knew without a doubt that this was the man I was going to marry. As he walked me to my car, I was dying for him to ask for my number, to say he wanted to see me again. We stood outside in the bitter temperatures, freezing and shivering, sharing formalities, but he wouldn't ask me! But, finally, he asked. At that point, I couldn't stand outside anymore, so I abruptly handed him my business card and hopped in my car. Awkward, yes.

He didn't text me that night, and by the next morning at church, I had my phone out the entire time, waiting and waiting to hear from him. We finally connected and made plans to go see a movie that night. Then, later that week, we had a breakfast date. After that, we had our first real, just-the-two-of-us date at Gabriel's, a fancy restaurant in Sedalia. It's right on the train tracks, and there I learned about his passion for trains. That was the first night he held my hand and the first time we kissed.

I was blown away by how perfect everything was. He quickly became my best friend, and we fell hard for one another. We said I love you after two weeks and were very serious from then on. After only a few weeks, he took me home to meet his parents.

When we arrived, his mom, Cheryl, answered the door. The way this stranger that I had never met in my life looked at me … the love in her eyes was the way I always hoped my own mom would look at me—even for just one second, just *one* time in my entire life. Then she opened up her arms and gave me the biggest hug.

I stepped into their house—a house with no demons or sin, a house that was full of love, kindness, grace, mercy, gentleness, peace, and all the fruits of the spirit. Somehow I felt, finally, that I was *home*, meeting a family that was everything I had ever wanted in my life. We had the nicest dinner, during which I learned about all of David's aunts, uncles, and cousins and heard their family's history. After that dinner, merely three weeks into dating, I just *knew* that this was it for me.

Before we went into his house, David had given me a warning: "If my dad says something funny or acts kind of off, it's because he has Alzheimer's—don't read into it." Then I fell in love with his dad, Ron, straightaway. He was sweet and so full of life, had such a big heart, and loved music, just like me. We always had music cranking, singing along with Journey and Styx at the top of our lungs, hitting all the high notes.

David was calm, loving, and patient—everything the scripture says about love—and had no idea what to do with me. He says I was the most exciting thing that had ever come into his life. When we met, I was all over the place: a high-risk entrepreneur, on TV, hosting a radio show, teaching dance. He's a very steady-Eddie, even-keel, daily-routine kind of guy. He's had Special K for breakfast every day since I've known him, except for the occasional weekend waffles and bacon, and has worked for the same company for twenty-two years. He loves living a very predictable life. We're so different and balance one another out wonderfully.

I fell for him hard right away and immediately saw such a future for us together. He became my best friend, and especially after meeting his family, I knew that this was the biggest gift I'd ever been given. I knew I'd met my future husband, and I was all in. I was used to moving fast and had kissed so many frogs by that point that I knew I'd found my prince. It was a sure thing for me, and I wanted to get married right out of the gate.

He, on the other hand, hadn't done a lot of dating and wanted to slow things down. He was always telling me he didn't want to mess it up and that we needed to establish a good foundation. We also decided early on that we were going to wait to be intimate until we got married. I had just become a Christian. I was fully invested in turning my life around, and I wanted to do it God's way. I'd screwed up a lot of things in my life, including relationships. I'd had so many false starts, and this was something that I was passionate about, so I didn't want to mess it up either.

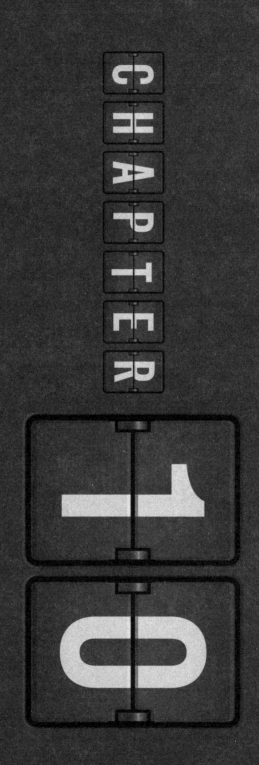

CHAPTER

10

CHAPTER 10

I was still living in my stinky low-income apartment, but the $500-a-month rent was great. I was still trying to get Million Dollar Butterflies off the ground, and David gave me a lot of support. We'd go straight from church to Starbucks, plan out the show notes, then head straight to the radio station. While we recorded, David would sit outside the studio with Rylie's mom, Julie, and they became fast friends. Creating that show was one of the greatest highlights of my life—I loved Rylie and our thirteen-year-old cohost, Josh. For the first time, my life started to feel so pure, safe, and protected.

Coming to the Lord and accepting him as my savior was the greatest decision I ever made. Week by week and day by day, going to church and diving into the Bible, his love and plan for my life started to be revealed. That time also revealed how hurt and broken I'd been. Little by little, I started to learn that only his love can fill those gaps, and that everything offered by this world can only offer temporary solace. Everything of the world that I thirsted or hungered for to fill the holes in my life—success, fame, money, recognition, rankings, or the spotlight—were ultimately of no real use.

Instead, I pursued prayer, worship, and quiet time studying the Word. He was very slowly starting to open my eyes and teach me about obedience and service—serving him and serving others. As I learned about his love, it transformed everything I ever understood about love.

After many more months without communicating with my family, I arrived home shortly after Mother's Day to find a dozen boxes sitting outside my apartment. My parents had emptied their house of everything related to me and shipped it, en masse, to my address: every picture, every video, every piece of pottery I'd ever made, the box of things from the hospital from the day I was born, my birth announcement, all the cards people wrote my mom congratulating her for having me, my baby book, framed pictures straight off the walls—everything. I was stunned. They had fully erased me from their lives.

I was stunned. They had fully erased me from their lives.

I didn't know what to do. I was emotionally shaken and in total disbelief. I called David and told him what had happened, and he suggested I talk to his mom. Even though we'd only been dating a couple of months, I called her, crying, and asked if I could come over. I didn't know who else to talk to. Of course, she said yes. As we sat on her back deck, she listened as I bawled my eyes out, trying to make sense of being cut from my family.

Still, I knew there'd be a healing journey ahead. Right away, I was asking myself a lot of questions. *What did I do? What did I not do?* Had it been a mistake to stand up to my mom? If I hadn't, we might still have had some kind of relationship, but I would've continued to be miserable. I felt a growing sense of peace in realizing that I'd never have to deal with her wrath again, and I had to consider what that future would look like. I knew I had a choice: go down the dark path or take the opportunity to rewrite the book of my life.

Right in front of me, I had a new family that wasn't riddled by demons, alcoholism, and abuse. They were so loving and calm, and there hadn't been a lot of loving or calm moments in my life growing up—everything was always a battle or an issue or a situation. I don't remember a lot of moments of just *being*. With David's family, it was so wonderful to just sit around and enjoy one other's company. I could feel the Holy Spirit giving me peace and comfort, and somehow I knew that everything was going to be okay.

However, I was struggling and making a lot of rookie mistakes as an entrepreneur, especially financially. I didn't know how to price for my services, how to delegate my workload or allocate my time. I said yes to everything, and as a result, I was all over the place. I gave everything my best effort, but I was overextended, still dealing with court hearings, being on probation, going to random morning urinalysis appointments, alcohol classes, and therapy. Juggling everything was *hard*. Meanwhile, for every $8,000 that came in, $10,000 went out. After cashing in my house and 401(k) and spending all my savings, I was starting to rack up debt.

That summer, I decided to launch a Kickstarter campaign for Million Dollar Butterflies—it had really taken off, and I was connected with a producer out in Hollywood who was interested in picking up the show to stream online. In our early conversations, I tried to understand what it would cost to take production to a higher level, as well as what was required from a legal standpoint. Working with kids in the entertainment business is very expensive—there's a *lot* of insurance and extra steps to make sure that they're protected. I just didn't have that kind of income coming in, so I started to pour everything into raising money through the Kickstarter campaign.

In the end, we fell short of our goal, and Kickstarter is all or nothing. When it didn't work out, I was upset—I'd given it my all for months, and now I knew I had nothing but debt to my name. At that point, I could barely afford that smelly low-income apartment. I had started selling my furniture to pay rent—I can still remember selling off my couches, a table, and my bedroom set. After that, I had next to nothing left—just a mattress on the ground.

When my girlfriends learned about my situation, one said she'd let me live in her basement for twenty-five dollars a week. I couldn't believe her generosity. I told the front desk at my housing complex that I wasn't making any money and couldn't afford the rent. They had a waiting list of other low-income people hoping to get in, so they terminated my lease and were happy to get someone else in there right away.

I knew that I needed to put dance on the shelf, keep consulting on the side, and most importantly, find a real job. I'd met a guy named Kris in my alcohol class, and when I'd asked what he did, he'd said he was working in tech and was the VP of sales for a managed service provider and data center. I still didn't know a lot about technology, but I knew I *really* needed a job, so I resolved to figure out how to get it.

They didn't have any open positions, but Kris said they'd be open to hiring a salesperson. As I was brainstorming how to get their attention, Rylie the superteen once again swooped in to save the day. When I asked her for a creative way to get the CEO's attention, she suggested we make a video. We went out and bought a bunch of posterboard and markers and made one of those videos to music where you gradually reveal a message through a sequence of cue cards.

I did research on the company and the industry, crafted a pitch, uploaded the video to YouTube, and sent it to their CEO. I offered to work for a $55,000 base salary, which is low in tech—most tech salespeople came in at $75,000 to $100,000, if not more.

That, combined with my enthusiasm and track record of success at PayCo, made hiring me a no-brainer. I still remember how excited I was the day that I got that job. I knew I was going to be able to start building my life back up, paying my bills, and getting out of debt. I knew I'd get commissions and that I'd probably be able to keep Million Dollar Butterflies afloat while continuing to finally, truly break into consulting. The idea was to only do sales short term and refocus on my business.

That, combined with my enthusiasm and track record of success at PayCo, made hiring me a no-brainer.

By golly, did I get involved with an awful company. Their work culture was so toxic. It was one of the most disgusting sales environments I've ever been a part of—constant inappropriate, demeaning comments about women. Even Kris from class ended up being a horrible, verbally abusive man. His game was to aggressively flirt with women to build them up and then tear them down by saying something mean and hurtful. Most of the women would instinctively want to get his attention back, so the pattern would repeat and escalate over and over. I watched this push-and-pull game play out over and over—it's the exact kind of behavior that I would've fallen for in the past.

Now, watching it from the outside, it was startling to see it happen to others. One woman in particular was falling for it, and I tried to give her counsel: don't feed into that! Her response was, *Well, you just don't understand,* but did I ever. It drove a wedge between us, and she grew to be pretty nasty toward me. With each day at that company, I felt more and more like an outsider. Their culture was *Work hard, play hard* all over again, but this time I knew I wouldn't fall into it.

Two events made me know beyond a doubt that I couldn't be a part of the company. The first was right around Halloween, when the opening slide in our regular 4:00 p.m. Friday sales meeting with a slideshow of women in quasi-pornographic Halloween costumes. The two men running the meeting were laughing and commenting on each new slide, and I felt disgusted to be even a tangential part of it.

Not long after that, the CEO booked a trip for all the employees to go up to Breckenridge to celebrate a milestone anniversary for the company. They rented multiple ten-bedroom mountain homes with bunk beds, and fifty or so employees came up. I wanted no part in all the drinking, mind games, and general debauchery, so I went back to my room early and wanted to just lock the door and hide. I was texting David about how startlingly different I felt—the old Mary would've been down there slamming shots along with everyone else. Now, I could barely stand to be adjacent to that culture, let alone partake in it. I knew I had to get out.

But there was a problem: I still *really* needed the money. I decided to approach a hardware vendor in the IT industry called EMC, whose products I was already reselling, and I sought an interview with them. After getting myself in front of their regional manager, I not only had a job offer but one with a much higher base salary—more than enough to comfortably live on.

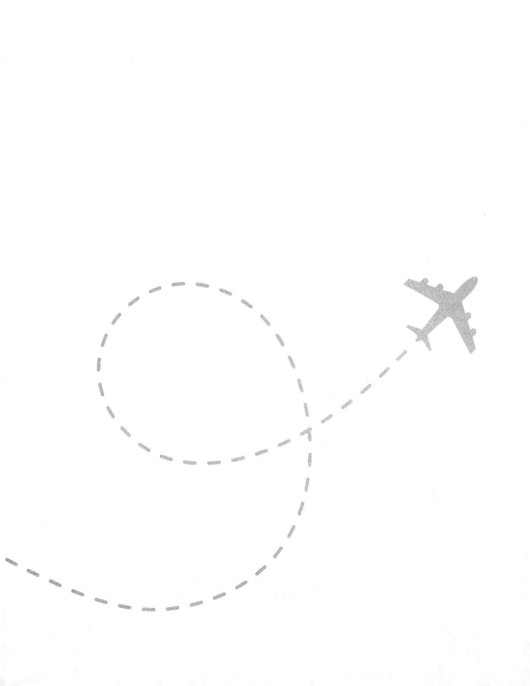

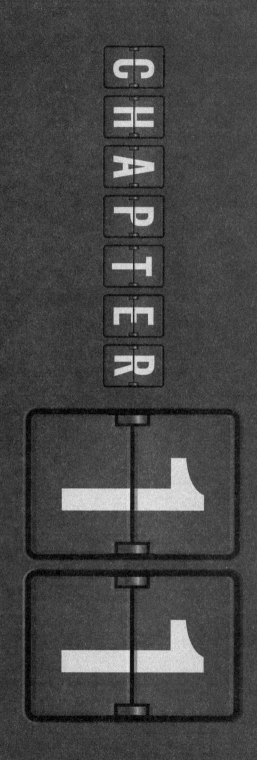

CHAPTER 11

Finally, I had enough money to get my own apartment again. I put down a deposit on an apartment in Lone Tree, and lived in my friend's basement as the complex was being built. It was a beautiful apartment, and the amenities there were extraordinary. I was so fortunate to have a brand-new place—I was the very first person to live there. It was also at garden level, so I was finally able to have a yard for Mister.

I was so excited, partly because I'd been on such a wild ride. It was a big deal when I moved in—it really felt like a rebirth. I'd been sober for a year and a half and gotten a full-time job while running my own company, and David and I had been together for just over six months. Everything was going extremely well, and I felt like my new life was finally starting. I had Jesus in my heart, money in my pocket, and a roof over my head and was getting serious with the love of my life. I felt unstoppable.

By the time my thirtieth birthday rolled around, I was growing closer and closer not only to David but to his family too. When I learned that his dad's sixty-third birthday was two days away from mine, we decided to have a joint "ninety-third" birthday party and invited all our friends. We got a DJ to run karaoke for us and set out a nice spread of food and drinks, and everyone brought us gifts.

As always, Ron had music flowing in and out of him and loved singing at the top of his lungs. Alzheimer's patients struggle with memory, but they don't forget music—the lyrics to the songs they love are among the last things they forget. Even though Ron's memory was rough and he couldn't recognize or remember everyone, the man sure loved music as much as ever.

At the end of the night, both of us sat at a table to open presents. Everyone was so generous and showered me with one gift after another for my new apartment. David's mom got me a hot-pink Keurig coffee machine, and I used it for years until the day it died. I can still remember taking all the gifts back home after the party, with David's family helping me carry them into the apartment, and how grateful I felt.

I felt so much love that evening—I'd never had a birthday party where I'd felt so loved and cherished. No one got mad at anyone else. Nobody was gossiping. Nobody got stupid drunk. It was just good people with good hearts, and they already felt like family. It felt like a window into the rest of my life. In a way, it all still felt a little foreign to me, but it was still so beautiful that my heart was overflowing.

Right around that time, I got a call from my oldest sister, Lisa, whom I love so much and who had raised and mothered me in my childhood more than my mom. I hadn't seen her or anyone else in my family since that horrible trip back to Indiana, let it go to voice mail, and called her back the next day.

We then proceeded to have a very strange conversation. It started out with one of us saying, "I haven't heard from you."

"Yeah, I haven't heard from *you* either."

This kicked off an argument, and our conversation went down a bad path. We'd only ever had tremendous love for each other, but this time it was different. She was very upset with me—a year had passed since my accident, and it had driven a wedge between us.

She told me that it was always difficult when I wanted to come see her because she felt like I was an awful example for her kids. Granted, in my twenties, I'd taken a couple of road trips out to see her and my family back in Indiana, all while still broken and unwell. I was still drinking and smoking, had no filter, and was cursing like a sailor. We'd be watching a movie as a family, and she said she'd look over my shoulder, notice what I was sending back and forth with friends or boyfriends, and thought it was all highly inappropriate. She told me I was living a reckless, ridiculous life, and that she didn't want me around her kids. The night of my DUI, she was the first person I called, and it didn't help that one of her kids answered in the middle of the night.

I felt like if I would ever have a relationship with someone in my family, it would be with her. We were the closest, and we'd been through so

When I started to talk to David about it, I gave him the first glimpse of the level of toxicity in my family.

much together, but on that call, we hurt one another deeply, and to this day it's still the last time I've spoken to her. It broke my heart, and I left the conversation very upset.

When I started to talk to David about it, I gave him the first glimpse of the level of toxicity in my family. I'd never sat him down to tell him about my past because I'd always been afraid of scaring him off. Every time I'd tell David little stories, he struggled to even wrap his head around what my life had been like. I knew I had to go easy on him because he had been raised so conservatively—the things I'd been through would've made his head spin. For a long time, I tried to keep things vague. I'd say that I'd had a really troubled life but had turned things around—I'd become a Christian, given my life to God, and lived for him ever since.

After Ron's party, I got to experience my first holiday season with David's family. The Saturday before Thanksgiving, they always have a ritual celebration called Pie Night, where they invite everyone they know, and everyone brings at least one pie. Anybody who wants to come can come, and it'd been a tradition in their family for decades. There are some light savory snacks around, but basically everyone's expected to show up and eat an embarrassing amount of pie, with no guilt.

Meeting David's family was an opportunity for me to dress up, which I *love*, so I bought a new black-and-white dress, did my hair, and got to look fancy to meet the rest of his extended family and their friends. I had the time of my life, and it was such a rebirth for me in terms of what constituted partying or having a good time—without drugs, alcohol, bad behavior, or a general atmosphere of sin. This was just love, fun, family, good times, singing, and praising one another—all of which was so different from what I knew. I'd never had a family gathering where people weren't at each other's throats or without someone ending up in tears and storming out.

This was followed by Thanksgiving proper, yet another tremendous evening with the family. Everyone was so genuine, curious about getting to know me and asking all kinds of questions. It was all the more special when I compared it to my previous Thanksgiving, where my family had treated me like I was invisible. Now I felt loved and cherished, at the side of the man I'd waited my whole life for. I felt so grateful just to be holding his hand and nuzzling up next to him in the presence of his wonderful extended family.

Throughout the holiday season, as things continued to progress unbelievably well in my personal life, I was also feverishly diving into God's Word and reading the Bible, participating in the women's ministry group, and going to church twice every weekend. David and I each had a church that we loved, so we went to one another's—first on Saturday afternoon and then on Sunday morning.

I absolutely loved that season of my life, learning about God, Jesus, the Holy Spirit, Christianity in general, and what it meant to surrender. I always found the scripture to be so peaceful, easy to follow and understand. I loved growing in my faith, and I loved the people I was surrounding myself with.

Faith and family started to come first. Throughout my twenties, it had been all about my career, working until I collapsed, cycling through burnout, and trying to win at all costs. It was amazing to put career second, make steady money, feel like a normal person, and grow in my faith. More and more, I wanted to take the next step with David. I wanted to get engaged, and started planting those seeds with him and our friend Sarah, the one who'd introduced us. I knew he was my forever, and I could feel him coming around too.

We had yet another wonderful day with the family over Christmas—again, a total reversal of the year before, when I'd woken up alone, cried in the booth at Village Inn, sat outside in the freezing weather, and become a Christian for the first time on the floor of my friend's apartment. Here I was, one year later, fully redeemed, and life was so beautiful. Perfection. Not a care in the world. God had restored everything in my life and was showing me what it looked like to be on his path.

After the amazing joint birthday party, I wanted to make sure New Year's Eve was just as special. I love New Year's Eve. Along with my birthday, it's my favorite day of the year. I'd always partied hard on both days—I've always loved to dress up, get my friends together, and dance until the sun comes up.

I asked David if he wanted to go out for the night, and he said yes. We booked a hotel room downtown, got tickets to a fun party, and made reservations for a fancy dinner. We got dressed up and went out to a restaurant called Oceanaire for dinner—I love seafood, and we had an unbelievable meal. I spent the whole night staring into David's eyes. As we were about to order dessert, the waitress put an ornate box in front of me. It looked like the kind of thing that would have chocolate-covered strawberries or truffles inside it. My first thought was, *How cute is this?* I thought the restaurant was giving us little complimentary to-go desserts for New Year's Eve.

When I pushed it aside, David started looking at me funny, like I needed to open it. When I started to, he got up from his chair, came over next to me, and got down on one knee. Everyone on our side of the restaurant started staring at us. Of course, I started crying. He pulled a ring out of the box and asked me to be his wife. I said yes and gave him a huge hug as everyone applauded us. When we left the restaurant and stepped out onto the Sixteenth Street Mall, it was still ten or so minutes to midnight, so we called his mom. She'd known all along and was so excited for us. When we got off the phone, the fireworks started instantly. Magical.

After that, we went back to our hotel room, played some music, and danced until falling asleep. That night I went to bed with so much peace in my heart. I knew that God was fully taking care of my life, and that I just didn't have to worry about it anymore. I didn't have to fight the way that I'd fought my whole life and could just fully surrender to him.

As I went to sleep that night, I was thinking about the year to come. The past year, 2013, had been one of the greatest years of my life. Blessing after blessing. God had taken such good care of me that year, and only he knew what was in store for me in the next.

When I woke up the next morning, I had so much peace in my heart and knew everything would be okay. We drove back to David's mom's house in the morning to pick up Mister, and when we came up to the front door, I found it so wonderful to see how happy she was to be gaining a daughter. As I was looking back at her, I knew that this was everything that I'd waited for—I was gaining a mom who loved me, and everything was about to change for the better.

It took her about two seconds to ask if we'd picked a date and if I knew who my bridesmaids would be. We both just laughed, and David asked if we could just be engaged for a minute. It wouldn't be long before we started planning the wedding, but for that day, we just relished the moment.

I made a commitment to David that I'd enter our marriage debt-free, so as 2014 got rolling, I focused on paying off my business debt. I was still working for EMC and doing very well, and though their culture was a lot better than my previous job, it still wasn't great. More and more, I found that I just didn't like selling IT to a bunch of men. A lot of IT companies have huge budgets and strongly encourage their salespeople to wine and dine prospects—in fact, if I spent less than $2,000 a month on my corporate card, I'd get flagged for not doing enough networking. My job meant constant lunches and dinners and taking one prospective client after another to sporting events.

I hate to speak in stereotypes, but bless their hearts, my IT manager clients were usually scruffy, nerdy men who hadn't exactly been socialites in school. I got the feeling that they hadn't had a whole lot of opportunities to go out with pretty girls, and more and more, I didn't like the way that I was being looked at.

I was always wearing my standard sales uniform—conservative, but skintight. I definitely looked the part—I had enough money to buy good clothes and was always dressed up and looking great for work, and sometimes I could just feel my prospects looking at me in a way that wasn't appropriate. I didn't want to be in an industry where

I didn't want to be in an industry where I was expected to take men out for a living.

I was expected to take men out for a living, especially as I kept growing in my relationship with my fiancé.

To make matters worse, I'd also started having strange digestive issues— I'd wake up with a flat stomach, then by noon or one o'clock my abdomen would be swelling up like I was six months pregnant. It was all very strange, and the swelling would bring a lot of pain along with it. First, I took allergy tests, and failing that, I started to clean up my diet. I tried cutting out gluten, then meat, then dairy, then sugar—you name it. It all helped, but not enough. Even after cutting out the obvious suspects, I'd eat something random, like an avocado or some popcorn, and swell right back up.

The pain became increasingly difficult to deal with, and it was even more frustrating that I couldn't figure out what was going on. I started trying different probiotics and kept going to the doctor, and they just kept telling me to cut out more and more foods. Nothing seemed to work consistently. It was embarrassing to be engaged, wanting to dress up and look cute to go out with my fiancé, and flat-out not being able to. I especially hated when the swelling became so uncomfortable that I had to cut dates short. I just never knew when I'd have a reaction and started to wear baggy clothes so I could conceal and hide the swelling.

As I kept trying different things, I started reading online about a condition called small intestine bacterial overgrowth, or SIBO. I went to a gastroenterologist and told them I thought I had it, and they said I was probably right. In the meantime, I started cutting out breakfast, since I usually started swelling up right around lunch. As I was running out of viable options of what to safely eat, I started to live off protein drinks. On top of everything, I was still teaching dance part time and burning calories like crazy, so I was hungry all the time and losing an unhealthy amount of weight.

We continued planning our wedding all along, and ultimately picked September 27 as our date—it was the only week David could take off work for our honeymoon. I wanted the wedding to be small, and mercifully, Cheryl is a way better planner than me. She tackled a lot of the details and even graciously offered to help us pay for it, as I was still so maniacally focused on paying off my debt—in the end, I was doing well enough for EMC that I eventually paid it all off.

Until the end, I loved living in that new apartment. It had an amazing gym and a pool, and at EMC I was able to work from either my home or the office. Most days I'd just roll over between seven and eight, work out, do my morning emails and calls, shower and get dressed, and run off to a few in-person appointments. When I didn't have meetings, I just worked by the pool.

I loved the flexibility of my career, and though I didn't love the job in and of itself, I still happened to be doing pretty darn good in my role. But as we started to get closer to the wedding, I started gunning for the door. I knew I didn't want to stay in that job long term, and I couldn't help feeling more and more uncomfortable wining and dining men day in and day out. I was about to marry the love of my life and wanted to devote myself fully to him.

I decided to see if PayCo would take me back. I called my old manager—not my ex, but my other manager, who'd helped me leave my husband and move out of my apartment—and he agreed to meet me for lunch. Let's just be honest: we hadn't parted on the best terms. By the time I'd left the company, I was a mess. But in the end, I'd been working with him when I was twenty-two and was now thirty and about to get married.

Thankfully, he still had great admiration for me as a salesperson and as a human. I told him what I'd done in the meantime and that I could come back ten times stronger. I laid out how I'd cleaned up my life and generally convinced him that I was no longer a complete handful. Their downtown Denver territory was open, and I knew I could come in and crush it. After thinking it over for a moment, he looked at me and said, "You know what? Let's do it."

My base salary dropped from $84,000 down to $47,000 a year, but I couldn't have cared less. I knew I could sell payroll in my sleep, my debt was paid off, and I was about to move in with my husband. I decided not to renew the lease on my amazing apartment when the time came, moved most of my stuff into David's house, then packed a few suitcases and stayed with my in-laws for the last month before the wedding. Everything seemed to be coming together.

My friend Sarah was my maid of honor, and she threw a bachelorette party for me up in Breckenridge. David's parents had a timeshare vacation home there, and Cheryl let us use one of their weeks. Five of us went up, and we had an unbelievable time—we had an amazing dinner, then went out and danced all night long. I was so grateful to have all these beautiful women in my life—most were just sweet married women with kids, and all of them also love Jesus. It was yet another glimpse of how it was possible to go out and party without being an idiot.

In the days leading up to the wedding, I couldn't help but look back and compare them to my previous wedding: my crazy, alcoholic mother ruining every day, a grandma hating me for my lack of planning, my dread of marrying an abusive man that I had no reason to be with, and a general feeling that I was doomed.

Nine years later, I had everything going for me: I was about to marry the love of my life, on the verge of becoming part of the greatest family I could ever hope for, going back to a job I knew I'd be wildly successful at—all the while being surrounded by people I love who took great care of me. I felt like I had a second chance at everything in life.

At our rehearsal, my heart was overflowing. Not one thing went wrong. Everyone whom I loved and adored was there to celebrate with us. Meanwhile, not a single member of my own family knew that I was getting married. Not one: brother, sisters, aunts, uncles, cousins, nieces, or nephews. The only people present from my previous life were Rylie and her mom; my friend Vicki, who had been around since even before my DUI; and Anna and Christina, a couple of my friends who also taught dance. There were seventy-five people in the room, and only five were from the time before my rebirth.

I felt like I had a second chance at everything in life.

I looked out at all the beautiful faces and felt so grateful knowing that they would be the people who would carry me through the next stage of my life. Ron walked me down the aisle. When I stepped up to the altar to look into the eyes of the man I was about to spend the rest of my life with, there was not a shred of doubt in my mind. We professed our love for each other, then made our vows in front of God. It was the most perfect wedding I could have ever asked for. When we walked down that aisle on the way out, I just knew that this was *it*.

We got into our getaway car and drove off toward Sedalia. It's a gorgeous drive with views of mountains, hills, and valleys, and all the while, the sun was setting. We rode up the Santa Fe Drive through Castle Rock, Castle Pines, and into Sedalia, where we had our reception at Gabriel's, the same place we'd had our first real date. It was truly one of the most magical nights of my life—exactly how a wedding should be.

After the reception, our friend drove us up to our hotel for the night. I knew how special it was going to be, because we'd kept our commitment to wait for marriage to be intimate. Even though I was thirty years old, I felt like this was a second chance for me to start my marriage God's way. I wanted to invite God into our marriage in the purest form, to dedicate and surrender our marriage to him. It was an unbelievable evening together, one that I will absolutely never forget.

We stayed at the Hilton Denver Inverness hotel, and that next morning we invited our family and friends there for brunch. It was wonderful to see everyone and celebrate the day. When everyone went back home, we had to pack our bags for our honeymoon in Cancún, where we stayed at an unbelievable private five-star resort for a week. We had a lot of nights where we'd just sit out on the end of the dock with our arms around one other, swinging our feet, looking out into the ocean, and talking about the future.

In Mexico, I ate everything—I didn't try to limit my diet, and I never swelled up once. Their food is different from the food in America—I feel like what we have is poisoning and killing us through the way it's over processed and manufactured. I ate everything we were served in Mexico and never swelled up, never got sick, and had no digestive problems whatsoever.

When we came back, I was so ready for the rest of my life: to go back to PayCo, to move in with David and make his house our home, and for Mister to finally have a dad. From the second I set foot inside my new home, I fell in love with my life in a way that I never had before. I also started to fall in love with myself and began the process of forgiving myself for the hardship, the pain, the challenges, and everything else.

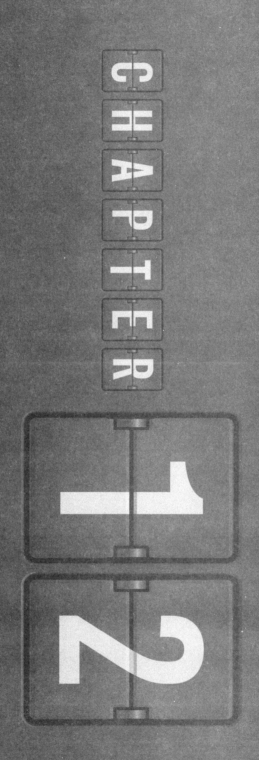

CHAPTER

12

CHAPTER 12

New house, new husband, new last name, new job. I was so excited to go back to PayCo, but all over again, I was also a little nervous. I didn't know how much the people there remembered my days as a hellion, and I was worried about what they'd think.

Thankfully, there'd been some turnover, and there were plenty of new faces on the team. Working with my same old manager was very comforting, because he and I had such a long history and solid relationship. He knew I'd made a lot of changes and cleaned up my life, and it was clear that a very different person was walking through the doors this time around. The old version of myself had died. I was truly a reborn individual and held my head high when I showed up, thankful for the new relationships to be made.

It was quite something to walk through the very same front doors that I'd walked into as a twenty-two-year-old. I felt like a kid on the first day of school. All over again, it gave me an overwhelming feeling of comfort. I felt like I was coming back home. PayCo had raised me professionally at a really hard time in my life, and I was so grateful for the opportunity to come back.

It was lovely to meet the new people, set up my desk with a new last name, and arrange photos of the completely new people in my life—I couldn't help but take a picture and send it to my husband. I'd been gone for three and a half years, and it took all of an hour to get thrown fully back into the maelstrom—my manager wasted no time in bringing me onto a call for a client who had terminated service and was looking to come back.

I was a little bit nervous because I hadn't sold or represented the product or service in years, and our technology platform was brand new. While I was away, the company had invested in a new, homegrown payroll platform, and I hadn't learned or even seen it. Meanwhile, the Affordable Care Act brought a significant amount of business to the payroll and HR industry because of its new reporting requirements. There were a lot of businesses out there that didn't know how to comply, so payroll companies like ours had a really nice tailwind from that dramatic shift in the market. I was coming back to the fold right as we were selling quite a bit of new business almost without effort.

Nevertheless, it's always been important to me as a salesperson to be knowledgeable and able to answer every question. Many salespeople tend to say yes when they may not know something. The better ones say, "What a great question—I don't know the answer to that, but I'll get back to you," and the *best* salespeople don't do either—they take the time to learn their product or service inside and out. I knew I'd need to know our product so thoroughly that I could be a one-stop resource for my prospects and clients. It's very powerful: it shortens the sales cycle, reduces friction in the buying process, and increases trust.

With that said, the fact that my manager threw me straight onto a phone call without knowing all the new ins and outs made me very nervous. Thankfully, our call went to the prospect's voice mail. I realized right away that I needed to get up to speed, and fast. I went online and started researching the ACA, figured out how what we were selling helped our clients, and did a deep dive into our systems. Throughout that week, I surrounded myself with peers who had been selling the new platform successfully, asked them a mountain of questions, and connected with the operations team to learn how I could best fill my role.

Once I had my bearings, I dug into the customer relationship management (CRM) system, looked at how things had been progressing in my territory, and started developing a sales plan. The fiscal year for PayCo starts June 1, partly because it's far easier to change payroll companies on January 1 than it is in the middle of the year. As a result, "selling season" in the payroll industry is October, November, and December. For many of my selling years, I did around 25 percent of my annual sales volume in January, so I knew how important this period was going to be. I'd come back in October—right into the thick of things.

Though my quota to make President's Club, the annual sales awards trip, was prorated, it was still a big number, and I was a little concerned about missing June through September. But I was a top rep. I knew it was attainable—I just had no time to waste. That first week of October, I decided, as usual, to tackle it all head-on. I hustled to learn my new **I poured everything into my new role.** territory, identified low-hanging fruit and other hidden opportunities, and mastered everything that had changed in my absence.

I poured everything into my new role. I got back into the habit of leaving the house early, getting to the office first, then simply getting things done: outbound prospecting, telemarketing, networking, cold calls. I would go around downtown Denver, walk door to door through all the office buildings, get kicked out by security, and did everything in my power to rebuild my pipeline. I absolutely refused to fail. From day one, I created a narrative in my head that I would be the comeback queen.

I'd left as PayCo's number one sales rep, and people had been shocked when I'd come back. There were a lot of eyes on me: *Can she do it a second time? Will she fail?* I loved channeling all that into motivation. I called everyone that I knew and joined every networking event I could cram into my schedule.

As I went all in at PayCo, I was loving my new life as a newlywed, and still managed to teach dance part time. It was an amazing autumn. By December, I'd built enough of a pipeline to do over six figures in January. There were some pretty large deals in there—many for companies with several hundreds of employees, and even one with a couple thousand. It was as exciting as ever to see my numbers shoot up on the leaderboard.

But it wasn't without stress and strain. Our new technology platform had issues, and more importantly, the ops team wasn't trained on it. As a result, after those first few whirlwind months, I entered into a very difficult and frustrating season. I'd worked my tail off to get contracts signed and new business in place, and when implementation and onboarding processes started in the winter, it was a total mess. Nobody knew what they were doing.

Before going out to sell, I'd taken the time to learn. I got a demo account, poked around, got a direct line to the sales engineers to ask technical questions, and really schooled myself in our system and its integrations. Payroll systems often have to integrate with proprietary and accounting systems, billing tracking software, and/or time and attendance software. It's very important to understand the integration capabilities if you're going to be an effective salesperson, so I made sure to work through things like general ledger exports, field mapping, testing imports, and beyond.

As I took the time to drill into all this, my counterparts in operations weren't given the same opportunity. They had more accounts than they could handle, and it wasn't their fault. Their email response time stretched from one to two weeks as their voice mailboxes filled to overflowing. They felt unsupported in the deluge and started to hate their jobs, and the whole situation turned into more and more of a disaster.

So there I was, optimistic and excited, hustling as always, pulling in contracts left and right. Then, everything started to fall apart—boy, was I upset. I'd been so passionate about making the commitment to perform and thought I was riding high in my relationships and building my stature back inside the company.

Everybody was impressed with my numbers, and people were reaching out from all over the country. When people heard I was back, they started following my progress on our CRM. As word got around that I was performing, more and more people were keeping their eyes on me.

Meanwhile, I hadn't fully healed from my addiction to success. In no time, I was thinking, *Let's show them all what this new married, Christian version of Mary is all about.* It started to expose the deep, dark holes inside me, where I still got a jolt from people telling me I had done a good job. I can't deny that it was still comforting and continued to propel me to perform.

When we started to have implementation problems, it felt like my world had come crashing down. My phone was ringing around the clock, and I'd be talking with new clients until ten or eleven at night. I continually had to pause my sales efforts to go on-site to help new clients onboard. Implementation was such a mess—our clients *and* our operations people needed help.

Because I'd taken the time to learn the technology and had five years in the company, I knew how to do implementations and understood them very well. Gradually, I didn't even have time to sell—I was on-site, inputting data, balancing spreadsheets, doing QA on imports, reconciling year-to-date taxes and payroll amounts, and hand-building integrations between accounting and payroll systems. It was a nightmare, and my manager told me, "You can't do that. You need to be *selling*."

My response was, "Selling what? An absolutely awful product?" I'd put my name on the line with all these businesses, and our operations team was crashing. Again, it wasn't their fault, and I didn't blame them. But in the end, they were failing us *and* our clients. I told my manager, "I will not sell until my existing clients get implemented."

December and January were difficult. I was on edge, stressed, burned out, and feeling more and more defeated. When I lost a couple of the clients I'd sold because the implementations were so bad, I started to consider that I'd made a bad decision to go back to PayCo, that I'd need to find a different job, and that I'd made a big mistake. I stopped going into the office and gradually withdrew from my role.

At that point, my manager had a very stern conversation with me. He told me, "I'm not paying you a base salary to sit around and *not* work. Either you need to get over this and come back to work or you can resign. Take a couple more days—do what you need to do to grieve, or be frustrated, or be mad at me or the company. I don't really care. Go do what you need to do, think it over. And I want a decision by Monday. You need to either commit to this role or hit the road. If you can't handle it, there's no longer a spot for you on this team."

That was all pretty intense, but I ultimately made the decision to pull myself together and stay in the role. I knew I could be successful with that company and that I had to give my operations team some grace. I also needed to take ownership of what I could have done differently during the sales process. I decided to show up on Monday, apologize to my manager for my bad attitude, and let him know that I was picking myself up off the ground.

Next, I came in with a plan and took full accountability for my sales process. At that point, I knew our system's limitations—what it could and could not do. I went back to my territory and our CRM,

I ultimately made the decision to pull myself together and stay in the role.

segmented by industry and company size, and found prospects who would be a good fit for our technology, imperfect as it was. I had to recalibrate and focus on not overselling. From there on, I only targeted people who were great fits. In taking ownership in where I could do better, I decided to focus on a slim, narrow niche of companies that I knew would have easy, seamless implementations. In turn, I restructured my prospecting plan and my list of target accounts. I also went back to the drawing board with my networking partners and met with them frequently, and together we built a pipeline.

In the end, I closed out the year strong, sold well above my quota, and did well enough in January to qualify for President's Club. By the end of April, I'd sold what I needed to close out the fiscal year strong—over $300,000 in revenue between February and May. I was really excited to have pulled off a win under the challenging circumstances.

As implementations got better and easier, I was able to strengthen my relationship with the operations department. I knew it was of paramount importance to be in sync with them and work together harmoniously. As with any human relationship, when you take time to honor, love, and serve people, and really seek to understand where they're coming from, the results can be powerful.

I knew they were pretty beat up after a rough transition to our new technology and onboarding all our new customers. I think it was refreshing for them to have a counterpart on the sales team that took the time to treat them well, build relationships, and be their partner, instead of just piling more work on them. Our improved relationship became the hallmark of the changes I'd made since leaving PayCo. Now I was a new woman with a cleaned-up life. How I interacted with people was completely different, and it really contributed to finishing out the year strong.

Then, of all things, I started to feel really conflicted by all my success. I was back to making a lot of money—on top of my base salary, I was easily receiving over $20,000 a month in commission checks. My pipeline was on autopilot, and I didn't even really have to work very hard.

Around that time, I took a trip to Breckenridge with my women's ministry group. We rented a large shared home and had a few days together in worship, prayer, fellowship, and the Word. A couple of guest speakers came through, and it was really a wonderful time, yet I still felt conflicted throughout and took the opportunity to dive deep into God's Word. We were doing a lot of activities together, talking about our callings, our lives, why we were created, and God's purpose for us.

As all this was going on, something hit me in the pit of my stomach. I felt like I wasn't sufficiently serving the Lord, hearing his calling for my life or living his plan for me. I felt somehow that I was making a mistake and wasn't honoring God in my work. I'd taken the easy path: going back to PayCo, selling what I knew how to sell, capitalizing on my great track record, and making a lot of money.

That's not what being a Christian is about. It was a hard realization, because by April, I finally felt like I really had it all: the husband, the job, the house, the money, the car, the friends, and an almost total absence of stress or issues in my life. Everything was good, and I felt undeserving of it.

If you read the scripture, you'll find that the Christian life is not supposed to be an easy life. Becoming a Christian doesn't mean that one day a fairy godmother bops you on your head with a magic wand and suddenly makes your life perfect—yet that was basically the life I'd found. The more I felt like I wasn't using my life the way God created me for, the more it gave me anxiety, and despite everything, I'd never really struggled with anxiety or depression that much. I'd had waves of it, but it was always triggered by concrete things, like my accident.

This was more of an existential feeling—being scared at who I was turning into and of dishonoring God in the way I was living my life. Yet at the same time, I also wasn't clearly hearing precisely what the Lord wanted from me. It was challenging, and it put me into a very funky, weird place, emotionally and spiritually.

All this was obvious—when some of the women started to ask what was wrong with me, finally, I just broke down. Again I had to tell someone: *This can't be what God created me for.* I'd said it that fateful Christmas on my friend's floor, when I was at the bottom, and now I was saying it from the top. I was on the easy road. I had so many talents, a fiery heart, and could take on a lot, yet I felt like I wasn't being used to my full capacity.

I got some mentoring from the women around me—they told me to enjoy a quiet season, one in which God was likely preparing me for what was to come. They told me to see this part of my life as a season of rest and encouraged me to take time to invest in my marriage and my career, save money, be responsible, love the people around me, dive deeper into the Word, and build my relationship with God. It would be wise of me to charge up for whatever came next, to confront it fully rested, prepared, and with more to give. I took that to heart, and though it sometimes felt too easy, I tried to deepen my relationships with my friends, my new family, my new husband, and God.

All the while, David and I had been nurturing a dream to move to Castle Rock, where David was already working. It's a cute little town, family friendly, with a beautiful little historic downtown that loves to shut down the streets for fairs, festivals, and fireworks. We saw a future there, maybe four or five years down the road, when we had a family. We dreamed of building a house there, and even found the very piece of land that we wanted to build on. We kept calling the city, trying to figure out when it would be developed.

One day, when David and I were driving through, we stopped the car, parked on the side of the road, and walked up a giant hill to an open space. There David told me, "One day, we'll have a house up here." The land opens up to an eastern view of a large valley and has a view of the actual Castle Rock for which the city is named. We wanted to be able to see it out the window of our future house.

That hill is also right on the train tracks, and again, my husband absolutely loves trains. He'd spent years and thousands of dollars building a full N scale train model layout in the basement of his first house, and he was even part of a model train group with his friends, several of whom also happen to be named David. It was a lifelong passion—he'd been building those layouts with his brother and his dad since he was a kid. The lot we wanted to build on was just a few feet from the southbound BNSF Line, and maybe a hundred yards west of the northbound Union Pacific Line. It seemed like fate.

Meanwhile, we still loved our house in Parker—a two-bedroom starter home, with a great lot, really well kept—David is a clean freak, and I love him for that. When we talked about planning our family, we knew we could at least have one kid in our Parker house, then move to Castle Rock if we were blessed with a second child.

David and I took a trip together to visit his brother Mark in New York City, and it was extraordinary. It was our first trip since our honeymoon, and New York always had a special place in my heart. We did all the touristy New York things: rode the subway, took pictures eating hot dogs, saw Broadway shows and the Rockettes, and took pictures in all the iconic places. I also happen to love *Sex and the City*, so of course we went to Carrie's doorstep and took a photo there.

It was wonderful to be able to further cement my relationship with my brother-in-law. Mark and I are actually very similar—we both thoroughly enjoy our careers, are corporate business oriented, and like me, he's embraced the intense peaks and valleys of his work. Mark is also quite the foodie and loves to travel, and, especially compared to my even-keeled, homebody husband, our personalities are similar. We all had so much fun, and I continued to appreciate how much of a blessing my new family was for me. I had a new mom and dad, and now I'd found a new brother.

A month after we returned from our trip, around Mother's Day, Cheryl's house flooded. There was a bad storm, her sump pump stopped working, and the basement was waterlogged. She lived in a big, beautiful home—at that point, way too large for what she and Ron needed. Meanwhile, Ron's Alzheimer's was progressing rapidly, and Cheryl had retired early to become his full-time caregiver. She'd been an accountant for car dealerships for the majority of her career, was amazing at her job, and had a lot more left to give. She was already taking on a lot around the house, and when the basement flooded, it just became too much. I think the weight of everything on her shoulders hit her hard, and she realized how truly too big their house was for the two of them.

All this escalated David's and my future plans, and we started looking for homes in Castle Rock far sooner than anticipated. Sadly, our dream lot was years away from breaking ground. After looking at a few houses and failing to fall in love with any of them, we found a lot that we *did* love. It was right next door to a brand-new mainte-nance-free duplex-condo living community that would be perfect for Cheryl, *and* an elementary school for our first child.

When the new fiscal year started at PayCo, our product progressively became more difficult to sell.

All of a sudden, we all went under contract, building two houses almost right next to one another. Ours was at the top of a hill, and you could roll right down it to arrive at Cheryl's. Our house was a little outside of our budget, and that made me nervous. When the new fiscal year started at PayCo, our product progressively became more difficult to sell. We'd mostly ridden out the wave of the Affordable Care Act, and a new competitor had entered the market and was eating up our market share. After finishing strong, I was struggling to start the new year off in the same way. That hit me hard, because it was still my first full year back. I was determined to be at least in the top five or ten, if not number one.

It all made me increasingly worried about affording our mortgage payment. I told David, "This isn't gonna end well." We'd made the deposit and all our design choices, but I didn't think we'd be able to pull it off. I didn't want to be overcommitted financially. My base salary was $47,000 a year, and David was making around $70,000. If things didn't go well for me for the entire year, it wouldn't be enough. I was the one with variable income, and at that point, I didn't see it happening. It was *not* a good feeling. I felt like I'd let us down. I felt defeated, like I'd failed myself and my husband. It'd been a long time since that old feeling of not being good enough resurfaced, and I wasn't happy to notice it creeping back in.

We went back on the market to see what was available for sale in the neighborhood directly next to our original dream lot and noticed a house for sale on a lot that flanked it. The view was absolutely stunning, and the cost was $150,000 less than the house that we'd committed to build. We went to look at it, and it was absolutely perfect. You could still see both train tracks from the house, and a train even came by while we were at the viewing, which we took as an omen.

We immediately put in an offer, negotiated, went under contract, and moved in that September. It was an immense relief. The price and location were perfect—two and a half blocks away from Cheryl. God came through in that moment to give us a blessing disguised as a defeat. I'm still grateful for this home, which, as I write this, we're still living in.

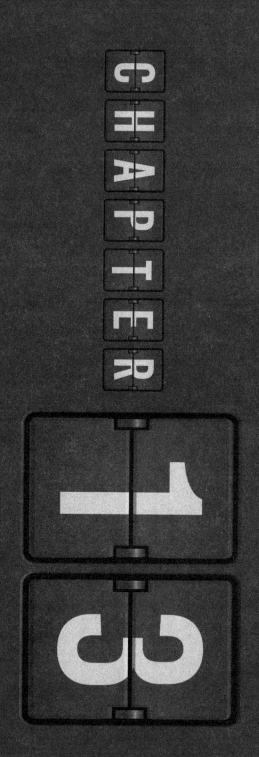

CHAPTER

13

CHAPTER 13

We were able to sell our house in Parker right when the market picked up, earned a lot more than originally expected, and moved in with Cheryl and Ron for about three months in the interim. From there, David went into Mr. Fix-It mode, doing repairs inside and out. We both pitched in on taking care of Ron, which took some stress off Cheryl's plate. It was a really sweet time. As we gave Cheryl the support she needed, our collective relationship grew. We became so closely knit, eating family dinners together almost every night. Ron was getting worse every day, but we'd still crank CDs super loud and sing along to all his favorites and did more puzzles in three months than I ever would've thought possible.

We closed on our house in September and moved in, which was hard for Cheryl, since her house wouldn't be finished until April. We promised to come by often to help, and did—especially on weekends and weeknights. Mark was still living in New York, but he also came back as much as he could—seven or eight times a year, if not more.

David and I had been trying to get pregnant for four or five months, seeing how it would go. We weren't unduly intentional or trying too concertedly to time things, but we certainly weren't trying to prevent it either. Then, when we got into our new home, we got a little bit more serious and intentional. Any woman that's gone through that knows it takes a toll on your mind, your heart, and your emotional well-being. We became quite serious with testing and timing throughout September and October, and by the time November rolled around and I still wasn't pregnant, I was starting to get frustrated.

I know plenty of women who have been in the same situation—it doesn't take long before you start asking, *What's wrong with me? Why won't God bless us with a baby? Is something physically wrong with my husband? With me? Our reproductive systems? What's happening? Why isn't this working?*

After months of frustration, I said to heck with it. My birthday was coming up, so I suggested we go *back* to New York City. We called Mark and told him we wanted to come back out and party. David and I booked a couple of flights, and we went and spent an amazing few days there, just having fun.

Shortly after we'd gotten married, I'd started drinking again. I was done with everything related to my DUI, in a much better place, living in a very protected environment, and in a loving relationship and wasn't contending with the stress, the negativity, or general woes of my twenties.

Now, I could handle alcohol a lot better—or so I thought. That's a lie that alcoholics tell themselves: *This time around, it'll be different.* I'd been sober for so long and wasn't drinking heavily—I'd have inter-mittent glasses of wine here or there, and it really wasn't affecting me. But when we'd go out and party in New York, I fell into a lot of drinking, partly out of being so frustrated with trying to get pregnant. We partied hard and ate a lot of delicious food, and it was generally a gluttonous time.

I think my body just needed that release. I needed to let go. By the time we got back, I realized that I needed to take myself less seriously—in general, with family planning *and* in my job. I'd been unnecessarily stressing myself out. And then, just like that, we conceived our baby. It's amazing how God works and how our bodies work. As soon as I just let everything go and wasn't tied to any outcome, everything just came together. I'm very in tune with my body, and I knew within a week—I could just feel the embryo trying to implant. Meanwhile, I was taking pregnancy tests every day, and they were all negative, because it was too early. But I *knew* something was different and changing in my body.

After a while, I knew I needed to go see the doctor—something was either terribly wrong or I was pregnant in a way that wasn't showing up on the test. I scheduled a doctor's appointment for the following week, and in the interim, I took a test that finally came back positive. I was so thrilled. I'd been saving a cute little "Daddy Loves Me" bib and a newborn outfit with a little train on it and packaged them up to give to David as a surprise. It was a very special moment for us to realize we had a baby on board and that we were going to be starting a family.

I had my first ultrasound on December 23 and got to see the little nugget growing inside of me. Everything was perfect—by two days before Christmas, I had the pictures of the ultrasound and confirmation of a strong heartbeat. I knew that on Christmas Eve I'd be able to tell the whole family that we were finally expecting. I wore a T-shirt that said "This Girl Is Gonna Be a Mommy," then covered it with a sweater for our big Christmas Eve party.

I waited until we were doing family photos in front of the Christmas tree, handed my phone to Cheryl, and asked her to take a picture of just me, David, and Mark. As she fiddled with the camera,

I took the sweater off. It was such a fun moment when she read my shirt, and everyone was there to share in the moment. I had my next ultrasound a week later, and everything was progressing well—all in all, an incredible way to close out 2015. Looking ahead into 2016, I knew a lot was about to change.

Soon, it did: exhaustion, morning sickness, and everything else that comes with being pregnant. Soon, it started to become a challenge to be at work. By New Year's Eve, I was only seven or eight weeks pregnant and thoroughly exhausted. Instead of partying, we just went to dinner with Sarah and Josh for an early New Year's Eve dinner at an Outback Steakhouse. I still remember feeling so blessed and grateful and praising the Lord for everything that he'd been able to do in my life that year.

The beginning of 2016 was exciting—I had another great January at PayCo, and Peyton Manning took the Broncos to the Super Bowl. David's parents have been season ticket holders for decades, and they passed their tickets down to David, Mark, and me.

My baby belly kept growing. I've always been pretty slim, and I've only ever put on weight twice: when I was married to my ex-husband, constantly drinking beer and eating fried food, and when I was leaning hard into partying and dating. Otherwise, I've been a size zero or two going all the way back to high school. Before I got pregnant, my doctor was worried that I was *too* thin and recommended that I put on weight. I'm a huge foodie, so that was music to my ears.

Initially, I thought my baby bump was really cute. Before my hips started expanding, I still had fun dressing up—my figure was still great, except for the prominent bump growing in front of me. Then, when I started to expand even more through my hips and thighs, it started to become harder to look at myself in the mirror.

For most of my life, I've never been kind to myself with respect to my physical appearance—it goes back to how I was treated growing up, on top of the pressure society puts on women to look a certain way. As I grew older and more conservative, I really struggled with how to view myself and the way that I dressed—it was always lurking at the back of my mind.

Being pregnant also started to make me self-conscious when I was intimate with my husband. I knew he saw me every day, whether it was in the shower or when changing my clothes, and it wasn't like I'd suddenly ballooned overnight. But because I really take pride in my health, wellness, fitness, and physique, I couldn't help but get more and more insecure about how my body looked.

My self-consciousness drove a bit of a one-sided wedge in our marriage, and it manifested physically in the form of an enormous, human-size, U-shaped full-body pregnancy pillow. As my belly grew, I needed more support when sleeping, but I resisted getting it because I really enjoyed snuggling with my husband. Up until that point, we'd been inseparable. We had nothing but each other and our jobs, were still infatuated, and did everything together. When we'd first gotten married, we hadn't been limited in the things we could do—if we wanted to travel, there wasn't anything holding us back.

Then, when I became pregnant, I was tired, didn't feel well for days at a time, had to take a lot of naps, and was often just plain uncomfortable, on top of feeling insecure with how I looked. It changed the dynamic of our marriage, and that was difficult for me.

When I finally broke down and bought the body pillow, the first night I used it, my relief was so enormous that it turned into excitement, because my body finally didn't hurt while I slept. At the same time, it was sad—it was the very first night that I couldn't fall asleep snuggled up in my husband's arms. Up until that point, every single night since we'd gotten married, I'd laid my head on his chest and sandwiched my body right next to his. There was so much comfort, closeness, and intimacy in that, and I loved it.

As much as that pillow gave me relief, I also felt like it represented a symbolic separation, and it made me resent the baby for coming between me and my marriage. This led to some dark, negative thoughts about whether we'd made a mistake in rushing to get pregnant so early. On one hand, we hadn't been married very long when we'd started trying, but on the other, we *were* older—my husband was nearly forty, and I was in my early thirties—we knew we couldn't wait too long.

Nevertheless, I started to question our decision and why I'd pushed so hard in the first place. Of course, I didn't feel like I could tell anyone any of these thoughts, because they'd make me seem like a horrible, wretched person. I'd already expressed frustration with trying to *get* pregnant, and now here I was, finally pregnant and full of regret. In the end I kept it all to myself, which is never healthy. For a time, it was hard for me to love my baby. To be clear, there *were* times when I really loved being pregnant, but deep down, I knew I wasn't ready to be a mom.

By April, GG's house was almost finished, and we started helping her move out of Highlands Ranch, where she'd raised her two boys and made so many memories. Right before she moved, Ron had a dramatic psychotic episode related to his Alzheimer's in which he became threatening and violent. This was nothing like the real Ron, who was the sweetest, humblest happy-go-lucky guy, but anyone acquainted with Alzheimer's knows that it can turn your loved ones into monsters in the blink of an eye.

It was becoming increasingly hard for GG (a.k.a. Cheryl) to take care of him—he'd refuse to take his medication and do spiteful things, which led to them getting in fights. He couldn't remember to wash his hands, ended up shaving off part of his eyebrow, and brushed his teeth with scalding-hot water—all of which sound like little things until you experience them. Through it all, GG was so gracious. I cannot believe she handled it all as well as she did, but she's an unbelievably powerful, strong woman, and she got through it.

After Ron ended up in the hospital after his episode, the doctors recommended that he move into an Alzheimer's-focused assisted care facility. In Castle Rock, there's a group that converted a handful of residential houses into homes for people living with Alzheimer's—it's an amazing setup, and there are caregivers living on-site 24-7. It looks a little bit like a nursing home, but it's great for Alzheimer's patients because it feels like home.

When GG sold the house in Highlands Ranch and moved to Castle Rock, Ron moved to *his* new home too. I can't imagine how hard that was—the two of them had an unbelievable marriage, loved each other very much, and had raised two incredible boys. They were both very hardworking, loving people, and I just can't imagine what it felt like for GG in particular at that pivotal moment.

We helped as much as we could with the transition and helping her move. In the end, she got settled and set up then decorated her new place beautifully, as always. We all went to visit Ron as much as we could throughout that summer, and GG went there several times per week to make sure he had everything that he needed. I had a huge pregnant belly, so it was always fun for Ron to learn, over and over again, that he was about to be a grandfather.

I was about to close out the year strong at PayCo—I qualified for not just President's Club but the second tier above that, which comes with a substantial bonus. I also knew I was due in August, so I really put the pedal to the metal before my inevitable maternity leave. By that point, I was used to dressing up for work, strutting through downtown Denver with my high heels and my briefcase. It had always made me feel important.

At five months pregnant, I couldn't fit into anything, felt insecure, and was not feeling pretty *at all*. Now I was wearing flats and *waddling* from appointment to appointment. It was certainly a new era for me and how I perceived myself as a professional. I still looked up to all the powerful women at PayCo, all of whom had the look, the car, the walk, the swagger—beautiful from head to toe. I felt like that was all taken away from me when I was pregnant.

I had a great track record in selling to larger companies, still knew the technology inside out, and was very excited to join the team.

Then, PayCo decided to build an upmarket division to target companies with 250 or more employees and brought in eleven of their top salespeople, including me, to form a new team. Because there are far fewer companies with that many employees in any given area, they widened the geographic territory to include the entirety of Colorado, which greatly expanded my referral networks. I had a great track record in selling to larger companies, still knew the technology inside out, and was very excited to join the team.

Then, when they threw a sales kickoff meeting for us, they brought in a "unified sales playbook" with instructions for how we were supposed to sell. We all found that laughable—they'd taken their top eleven highest-performing reps, all of whom had sold millions over many years, and given us a brochure telling us how to sell as if it was our first day on the job. We were all looking at each other, chuckling and rolling our eyes.

But there *were* some challenges in the upmarket, mostly because our technology was still not built to handle larger companies. While

PayCo was investing heavily in research and development to improve our product, they had a history of playing catch-up with the market. They'd typically wait until a competitor rolled out a feature that the market loved, then immediately rush to build it into their own product. As a result, we were consistently six to twelve months behind our competitors. Our first releases always had issues, which would only stabilize after months of working out the bugs with our existing clients.

As a result, I had to become a pro at selling what we didn't yet have. Despite the cheesy rollout, I was still thrilled by this new opportunity, and it helped take my mind off what was going on with me personally. I modified my prospecting playbook to aim at larger clients and started building a massive pipeline.

At that point, some businesses had started to follow labor laws to protect pregnant workers and were building out rooms for pregnant women and mothers in their offices, but PayCo was not one of them. In that season, I was no stranger to lying underneath my desk in my cubicle to nap when waves of numbness and fatigue came over me. If I didn't take those cat naps, I'd often end up in real physical pain. I wasn't always so fortunate to be at my desk—if I was out in the field, in sales meetings, or driving, I just had to push through. I often wanted to cry and give up. As I started to get into my third trimester, those waves started happening every single day, and sometimes twice. I started to work from home as much as I could.

I tried to do light workouts, but by that point my body was changing more rapidly than I could keep up with. I simply hated how I looked and started being harder and harder on myself. I can still remember shopping for a dress to wear to my baby shower in mid-June. I wound up so disgusted with everything I was trying on that the episode concluded with me in the dressing room in tears.

After finally finding a white dress that I thought looked decent on me, I saw the pictures from the event later and felt crushed—it looked horrible. More and more, I felt flat-out disgusting, and it continued to drive resentment toward my baby. Don't get me wrong—I loved the kid and was excited about becoming a mother. My struggle was in being okay with *what I had to go through* to bring a baby into the world. It was just so, so hard.

Yet, through it all, I was successful in securing over $200,000 in new revenue at PayCo in the first two months of the fiscal year. I knew I'd be able to go on maternity leave, come back, and hit the ground running with a solid pipeline. I was very proud of myself for achieving that. After the baby shower, I started full-on nesting. We built a bedroom fit for a baby boy, painted it blue, and put beautiful decals up on the walls.

David and I also planned a couple of babymoon trips. We went down to Colorado Springs, stayed overnight at a historic hotel, rode the narrow-gauge Pikes Peak Cog Railway train, and went to Kansas City for his annual train convention, where I found myself eight months pregnant and eating plateful after plateful of barbecue. I was pushing 170 pounds at that point, struggling to control my eating, and hated looking at myself more and more. I continued to try to work out. I can still remember being on the elliptical machine, praying to God to help me through my pregnancy.

I wanted to be a mom, and I wanted to have my baby, but I was also starting to realize how significantly my life was going to change, and I didn't know if I was strong enough to handle it. I didn't know how motherhood would affect my career. I still felt like the pregnancy was driving a wedge between David and me (though he'll probably be surprised to read that). It was an awful time for me, but no one noticed because I kept quiet about it. There's so much joy when someone's pregnant, and I just kept telling everyone how happy I was.

At the root level, I knew I was only a couple of months away from my life forever changing. I love to sleep, and hearing about how much babies cry day after day absolutely filled me with dread. I knew there was no way I could function in my career without sleep. Throughout my third trimester, I further questioned my life's calling—whether my purpose was to be simply selling payroll and making a lot of money and whether that was really all God had planned for me. My internal monologue was so negative, and although I was less and less kind to myself, I kept smiling at everyone, saying how wonderful everything was.

The Summer Olympics rolled around as I soared right past my due date, still pouring on the pounds. At a certain point it started to seem excessive, like something wasn't right. My belly already looked like I'd swallowed a watermelon whole, yet I could *still* not stop putting on weight. When I'd weigh myself, it amounted to a pound or more *every single day*. As I got into the 190s on the scale, I was astonished that I was about to cross into 200-pound territory.

Then, at one of my regularly scheduled doctor's appointments, they told me I had polyhydramnios syndrome, where there's too much amniotic fluid around the baby in the womb. I'd started overproducing amniotic fluid, which had caused me to gain a full twenty pounds in the span of two weeks. As it became unbearable to walk or even be around anyone, I started working from home full time.

My feet were so fat and swollen that I couldn't even wear my flip-flops for more than twenty minutes. I started avoiding even trips to the grocery store—my belly was sticking out like a sideways torpedo, and strangers would literally gasp when they saw me. They weren't intentionally rude, but they said things that weren't called for. "Whoa!

When *were* you due? How *many* babies are you having?" I felt like a beached whale. I definitely did *not* want my husband looking at me naked—I couldn't even look at *myself* naked. I simply could not believe what my body had turned into.

By that point, I was exhausted almost all the time. I was constantly falling asleep on the couch and could have snored through a jackhammer. I was eventually sleeping fifteen hours a day, and bubble baths were about the most strenuous thing I was doing while awake. I was doing everything I could to go into labor: running up and down the stairs inside the house, eating spicy food, walking uphill through the neighborhood with one foot in the street and the other on the sidewalk, basically trying all kinds of ways to make myself lopsided, anything to try to shake that baby out. My neighbors must have thought I was nuts.

Finally, I just couldn't take anymore. I raised my hand and said I wanted to be induced. I'd developed an umbilical hernia on the backside of my belly button, so the doctors were concerned about me pushing my intestines out during a natural delivery. They advised a C-section, and I was terrified at the prospect. We'd done labor and delivery classes, and learning about C-sections had absolutely terrified me. Thankfully, I had a wonderful girlfriend who'd just had her baby, and she told me the good, the bad, and the ugly about delivery that most people don't talk about—what to pack before going to the hospital and what I should do afterward from a healing standpoint.

We went to the hospital, and I remember watching Usain Bolt win his medals as I was getting induced for labor. I was so excited for the whole thing to be over. I was absolutely *done* with being pregnant and scared to death about leaving that hospital with the baby and having zero idea what to do. We induced labor in the evening, and afterward I was able to fall asleep. Nothing really kicked in contraction-wise until about four o'clock that morning.

When those started, they were outrageously intense. I have nothing to compare them to, since I've only had one child, but holy moly—I'd *thought* I had a high threshold for pain. During the first major contraction, I was standing up and holding on to the rolling machinery cart for dear life. I'd never felt anything like it, and it absolutely took my breath away. Everything I'd learned in labor and delivery class went straight out the window. They'd taught us how to breathe, but when the moment came, I couldn't breathe at all. For a while, my body was just frozen and shuddering in pain.

When that first contraction was done, I threw up in the trash can, looked at my husband, and told him, "You call that nurse, right now. I can *not* go through that again." It was the absolute worst pain I've ever been in in my life. At first I didn't think I'd want an epidural, so I considered the alternative option: laughing gas. My attitude was, *Please, just hook me up to whatever you can so I never have to feel that pain again.* In the end they got me an anesthesiologist pretty darn fast, and for that I'm still grateful.

I had to suffer through a couple more contractions before my epidural, and it was the biggest blessing I could ever ask for. It changed *everything* for me. All of a sudden, labor and delivery became *fun*: I was just lying back, watching the Summer Olympics, hanging out with my husband, having contractions and feeling none of them. No biggie.

At three thirty or so that morning, they said it was time to start pushing. I remember thinking, *Wow, this is great. I haven't even been in labor for twenty-four hours.* I was quite literally in labor and texting friends, family, and coworkers, just hanging out and watching the Summer Olympics. Everyone was asking if I was okay, and I'd reply,

"Yeah, everything's great! This is awesome," at which point everyone must've known I was on a *lot* of drugs.

When it came time to push, David was about to go downstairs and get a snack. The nurses stopped him at the door and told him he was needed to assist in delivery, then made him hold my leg. He looked back at them as if to say, *I did not sign up for this.* He was not planning on being a part of the process—he's a little squeamish, as am I, but he's a trooper. They asked him to just try one push. Of course, as soon as I started pushing, the baby was ready to come out. Our baby boy, Beckham, was born at 4:01 p.m., just over eight pounds and as healthy as could be.

Right after he came out, I had this panicked feeling. *Oh boy. My life just changed.* A wave of panic hit me to the extent that I was nearly numb. They laid my son on my chest after they cleaned him off, and at first, he just lay there—I couldn't even touch him. The nurse told me, "Mama, you can hold your baby—put your arms around him!" For a second, the shock was such that I simply did not know what to do. As I wrapped my arms around my son, an odd feeling came over me. I thought to myself, *Wow, I really* was *pregnant. There really* was *a baby in there, and I really* have *a baby now. I really* am *a mom. What now?*

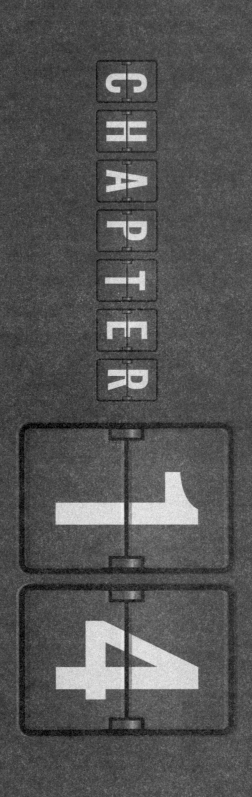

CHAPTER

14

CHAPTER 14

When you've gone through labor and an epidural, you don't feel the labor, but your body's still gone through it—it's like you've run a marathon. Like anybody else, my body needed to recover—and I needed to eat.

Cheryl was more than ready to come to the hospital to meet her grandson and graduate to her new grandma name: GG. She arrived with a wonderful surprise—Mark, who'd flown in for the occasion. By the time they arrived, everything had become a blur—I was very numb, and everyone was excited to see and hold the baby. Another realization: all the attention I'd been getting for the last nine months evaporated instantly. When you're pregnant, everyone wants to talk to you about the baby, put their hands on your belly, and constantly ask for updates and details. It's a *lot* of attention. In the hospital, I realized it wasn't about me anymore—I was no longer the star of the show. I was lying there, hating how I looked, body ravaged, clocking in at nearly two hundred pounds, in an increasing amount of pain, and entering into something I had no idea how to do.

When we all went home, I commenced a series of very difficult failures. One was figuring out how to nurse. I was able to get my son to latch on, but I wasn't producing any milk. The doctors said it would take time and to just keep up the habit, so for four days, I thought I was nursing and that he was eating, but no milk ever came out. With nothing going into his belly, he became jaundiced and lost weight. All babies lose weight after birth, but Beckham lost a *lot*. When we took him in for his pediatrician visit, the doctors immediately put him on formula. That baby sucked it down like he hadn't eaten in four days—which was essentially true.

When I realized I wasn't producing any milk, I really felt like I'd screwed up. I'd been so excited to nurse, then discovered I couldn't even feed my own kid. I was still in a lot of pain, and though my friend had prepared me for it as best she could, there are always things you take for granted, like being able to go to the bathroom normally or simply sit down.

I was extremely swollen, inflated, and generally *large*—when you have an epidural, they pump a lot of IV fluid into your body. My stomach had stretched out from all the amniotic fluid, and my body was a disgusting mess. Of course, everyone wanted to come over and see the baby, and I was mortified for anyone to see me. Then, when people ultimately did come by, they didn't even look at me—all the attention was on the baby, so I ended up feeling heartbroken that they didn't want to talk to *me*.

The first two weeks after the delivery were really hard, but thank God my son was a good sleeper.

The first two weeks after the delivery were really hard, but thank God my son was a good sleeper. He continued to be until about three or four months in, when you hit what's called the *fourth-month sleep regression*. In those first few weeks, he slept in a bassinet next to the bed, and then I was able to transfer him to a crib.

Two weeks after Beckham was born, we took family photos at Ron's new home. I could see that he was there, but he also wasn't there—his Alzheimer's had gotten progressively worse over the summer, which led to more and more medical challenges. He'd gone back to the hospital a few times and continued to struggle, and slowly, one by one, he stopped remembering who everyone was. By the time my son was born, Ron looked pale, lifeless, and nothing like his old self. I had a hunch that it might be the last time I'd see him. When I gave Ron a hug goodbye that day, something just told me it was our last time. As we started to walk away, I went back to give him another really big hug and told him how much we loved him.

A few days later, GG and Mark went over to hang out with him as usual. Mark had just been at the gym. When they arrived, Ron collapsed. By the time the paramedics came, he was sitting up and talking, and everything seemed okay. The paramedics laid him down and brought him to the hospital just in case, and on the way there he had a heart attack and passed away.

At the time I was at home with the baby, and David was at work. Cheryl called me and said we needed to get to the hospital right away—it wasn't looking good. I called David and let him know I was on my way out the door. When we got to the hospital, the scene was heart wrenching. They had done CPR for a very long time, trying to resuscitate him, but he was gone. I just sat there quietly with Cheryl and Mark, waiting for David to arrive. Because Ron had had a few of these episodes over the summer and recovered from each without issue, Dave had decided to finish up at work before coming. I had to meet him outside and break the news, and he simply could not believe it.

I brought him to the room, where we all just sat, mostly calling aunts, uncles, and cousins to break the news. Finally it became so intense that I couldn't bear to sit in there any longer. I took the baby out into the waiting area, and there, the craziest thing happened. I was absently looking up at the high ceilings when, all of a sudden, I heard Ron's voice. He told me, "Don't cry. Don't worry. Don't be sad. It's *beautiful* here."

A few days after she had passed away, my yiayia had visited me in a dream, and she had said the *exact* same thing to me: *Don't be sad—it's so beautiful here.* To hear that so clearly all over again gave me so much peace. I was so grateful that Ron didn't have to suffer anymore and for GG to be able to move on to the next phase of her life. She was healthy and had so much life ahead of her. She'd been in limbo as a caregiver for years, and now she could focus fully on being a first-time grandma and enjoy her early retirement.

All this had happened during my maternity leave. For all that time, PayCo had temporarily locked me out of their system, as was their policy for anyone on leave. I felt disconnected from my job, and gradually, panic and fear set in—I didn't know what was going on with my territory, my accounts, my pipeline, or anything. Then my manager gave me a call when he returned from the President's Club trip in Hawaii—one of my clients needed to be onboarded, and he didn't know what to do to move them forward, as I had all the details.

Something odd happened on that phone call—the old Mary came roaring back. I suddenly remembered that I was a talented, high-performing business development professional with an amazing career to go back to and that I needed to get back to work. The more I'd been hard on myself during pregnancy and struggling as a mom, the more the fire inside of me had died down. All of a sudden, I realized, *Wait, I am really good at something—here's something I can focus on and that I know really well.* Right away, I asked him how soon I could come back.

"Well, you have to take at *least* six weeks."

We made the plan for me to return in October, after just six weeks, and meanwhile, I worked with him behind the scenes to get that new client signed on. It was a rather large deal and put me in a very good spot for that year. Knowing I could go back to work early gave me a lot of peace. Work was comfortable for me—a place where I knew I could win and where I knew how to operate, regardless of what I was dealing with personally.

> **The more I'd been hard on myself during pregnancy and struggling as a mom, the more the fire inside of me had died down.**

We helped GG plan Ron's funeral, shepherded family and friends into town, and sorted through all the details for his funeral. It was wonderful to have the entire family together—that's the one blessing of a funeral. Once Ron was laid to rest, I started to get more in the groove of being a mom and found that I had a bit of a talent for calming Beckham down and getting him to fall asleep.

Eventually, I was cleared to start working out again. Once the swelling and inflammation cooled down, I immediately started dieting, going on walks, and being as active as I reasonably could. I was delighted when the weight came off quickly. By the time I went back to work, I was in the 160s, and celebrated by buying my very first pair of Spanx. There was no *way* I was going back to work without shoving myself into those things—they became a requirement and necessity for everyday apparel for quite some time.

At work, I hit the ground running. Childcare was a bit of an adjustment—we had a nanny three days a week, and GG watched Beckham the other two weekdays at her house. David and I split work duties, and I often worked from home with the nanny present to make sure I could pitch in where I could, because he was still such a little guy. On the days GG was on duty, I knew I didn't have to worry, and that gave me the opportunity to go hard at work. I was able to get my lucrative October deal signed and onboarded, closed a couple more deals, and loaded up my January pipeline. In no time I was closing at an unheard-of 75 percent rate, working on huge upmarket deals and solving complex problems—right where I love to be. I was back in business.

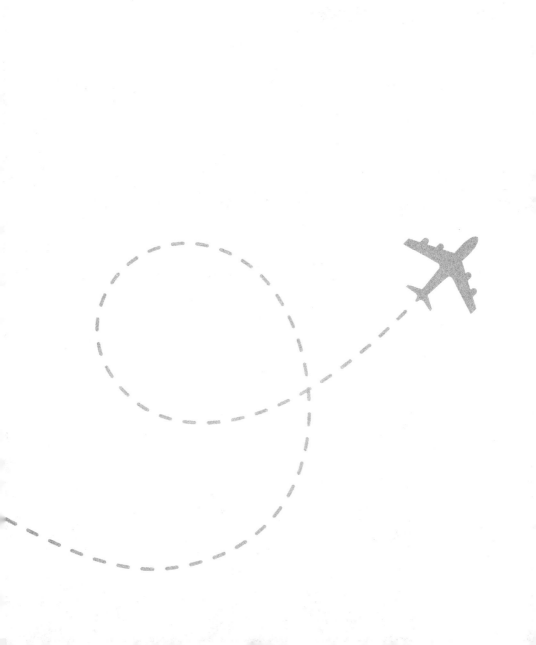

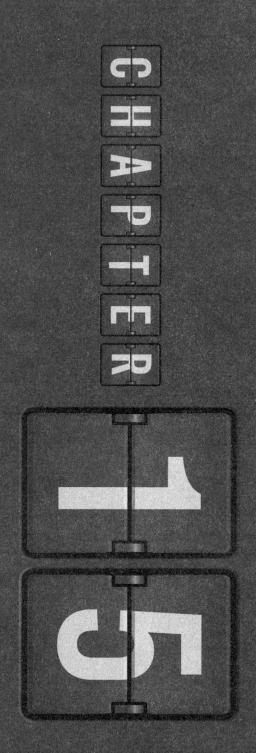

CHAPTER

15

CHAPTER 15

Then, everything started to vaguely annoy me, for lack of a better word. I developed a filter where it seemed like everyone was out to get me and was actively doing things to make my life worse—whether that be my husband, my son, my family, or people at work. I increasingly became frustrated with every little thing, yet somehow, on the inside, I still felt fundamentally happy. It was all very strange. Though everything was technically going fine, there was a persistent undercurrent of being irritated at everyone for making my life hard and purposefully stressing me out. All the while, my fuse got shorter and shorter.

I started to realize that something deeper was going on when we went to a routine medical checkup for my son, at which they suggested that he may need surgery. Though his condition and the surgery were fairly common, it all made me very nervous. He was only five months old, and I couldn't wrap my head around my little baby going under anesthesia. The earliest they could perform the surgery was at seven months, so we decided to wait another month to see if the situation would resolve itself.

That wait set my anxiety on fire. His surgery was scheduled for March 17, and by that time I was very much on edge—a walking cocktail of fear, pressure, tingling, numbness, and frustration, which made it very difficult to deal with anything else in a constructive manner.

In the meantime, a new opportunity presented itself at PayCo, a referral from a firm that assisted companies who were behind on their tax payments. They referred a five-thousand-employee company, which made it one of the largest potential deals that had ever fallen into my lap. My partner on the deal, John, usually sold to small businesses, so it was an even greater opportunity for him. We decided to tackle the contract head-on and set up a videoconference, and I steered the conversation toward a one-call close at full price. It was one of the top ten largest deals in company history, and we sold it at full price, no discount.

John and I both knew our company's troubled history with implementations quite well, so we promptly set aside everything else we were doing to ensure the deal's success. Our first order of business was arranging travel to Arizona. The client comprised 131 separate small companies, and each and every one had to be manually added to PayCo's system. When we got to Arizona, we were confronted with the most formidable stack of paperwork I've ever seen. It took the two of us an entire week working around the clock to get through it.

Back at home, Beckham got sick. David was doing his best to take care of him but had trouble adjusting to a schedule and knowing what and when to feed him. Beckham had just transitioned to eating things like scrambled eggs and avocado, but after I left, David put him straight back on the bottle. He was also putting him in clothes that he'd outgrown, which I'd see when GG and his nanny sent me photos each day. In the state I was in, seeing all this from afar made me continually livid.

Then, Beckham got a fever. By the time I came back home, he was burning up, wearing a little sleeping cap and footie pajamas that were so small that his little toes were curled up in the footies. I was so mad when I saw what was going on. I thought it was common knowledge: when your baby has a fever, you need to let the heat escape their body—you don't put them in a hat or cover their feet. I started ripping off his clothes to let him air out, laid him down in a diaper to cool down, then gave him his medicine.

From there, I absolutely laid into my husband, who just looked at me and said, "You can't have this both ways. You can't leave all week for work and expect things to be done the way you want them back home. If you want things done a certain way, you need to be here." In hindsight, I knew he was exactly right, but I was so mentally unwell and off balance that I buried myself in bed, crying, and refused to talk to him.

Week after week, I continued traveling back to Arizona, and before long it was time for the new clients to start running on PayCo's system—*and* time for my baby's surgery. I remember waking up nervous, fighting back tears, putting him in a little gown, and trying to stay strong. Because of the impending anesthesia, he wasn't supposed to eat. By the time we brought him in, he wouldn't stop crying, both from hunger and the unfamiliar environment. When they wheeled him back for surgery, I felt a piece of my heart go back there with him.

At the worst possible time, I started getting text messages from John back at the office.

Back in the waiting room with David and GG, I was a wreck—pacing back and forth and saying awful, negative things, just like my mother. Then, at the worst possible time, I started getting text messages from John back at the office. There was a disagreement between the regional managers at PayCo in terms of how we were going to split up our big new deal. Company policy stated that deals are to be split seventy-thirty: 30 percent to the referring partner (John), and 70 percent to the selling partner (me). In this instance, leadership was arguing over the deal because of its sheer size. The small-business team thought they deserved more, and unsurprisingly, the midmarket team didn't agree.

The small-business side drew a line in the sand: if I took 70 percent of the deal, then I couldn't work with John anymore. That, of course, wasn't going to work—John had become an integral part of the deal, simply because of the incredible amount of work we'd already done together. I knew the right thing to do at that moment was to give up 50 percent of the business to keep John in the picture, especially as I was sidelined with my baby in surgery.

So there I was, emotionally unwell, pacing back and forth, barking about an implementation deal in the waiting room in front of everyone. By the time Beckham came out, I was *still* making a scene. Everything had gone fine, but he was struggling to come out of the anesthesia—he wouldn't stop crying and just could not snap out of it. I remember holding him, burning up inside with everything going on.

When we got home and got him settled down, David noted how tense I was and suggested we get out for a night. GG said she'd stay overnight and take care of Beckham, so we went away and took the weekend to decompress. Our neighbor got us a deal at a fancy hotel, which came with several drink and brunch coupons. I put on a pretty dress, and we hit the hotel's happy hour, had a fancy dinner at a nearby steakhouse, and went out dancing—all in all, a fantastic night. I desperately needed to blow off steam and have some one-on-one time with my husband. I apologized profusely for my behavior, and he was clearly grateful to have snapped me out of my funk, if only momentarily.

However, partying and medicating through alcohol is not the solution to any emotional problem. That weekend of release bought us some time but didn't fundamentally solve anything. In the following weeks I continued to tell myself, *If you drink and party to blow off steam from the week, that'll make you feel better.*

On Monday, the clock kept ticking in terms of getting our new client launched before the fiscal year ended. I continued flying back to Arizona and trying to manage the rollout, but 131 entities and $800,000 in revenue is more than any one rep typically sells in a year, and we were trying to do it all in a month. Unsurprisingly, it was an absolute cluster. The deal was simply too big for my operations team to handle, and as always, it wasn't their fault.

I was on the phone with my regional manager, frustrated to the point of tears, well aware that we were in jeopardy of losing the deal altogether if we didn't manage to pull things together. Doing implementation work and helping a client run their first payrolls is definitely not in my job description as a sales rep, but after eight years with the company, I knew what had to be done.

It didn't help that I was absorbing the tensions of the employees of the new client I was helping. Many had been with that company for over ten years and were resistant to change. Our implementation issues were frustrating them to the extent that an employee of thirteen years resigned, which brought the owner of the company to tears. She came and told me, point-blank, "Mary, you're screwing this all up. I have employees quitting and even more threatening to quit. We lost one of our most valuable employees because of how awful this is."

Of course, I took that very seriously, but I also had to remind her how above and beyond our job descriptions both John and I were going. That's the thing about sales—you put it all on the line. If another part of your team isn't performing, the salesperson still takes the heat. I was staying up late, trying to keep things on track, to an extent that pushed me over the edge. Because of my company's inability to service our clients, I was pouring everything I had into trying to bridge the gap, all at the expense of not being home with my family.

Eventually, I reached a point where I couldn't do it anymore—by the end of April, I'd fully had enough. I was deeply unwell emotionally, increasingly unstable, questioning my career, and thinking about quitting PayCo, all of which made me horrible to be around. Somewhere around May 7, I woke up feeling the weight of the world. Nothing was right with work, and nothing was right at home. I was mad at David, at myself, and at life.

I took a shower, immediately started crying, and wound up sitting in the bottom of the shower until the hot water ran out. I simply did not know what to do. It felt like everything was falling apart. I contemplated quitting my job, running away, leaving my husband and son, and even ending my life. I didn't feel like I was doing anything right and didn't have the emotional or mental capacity to continue fighting.

When the hot water ran out, I wrapped myself in a towel, put on a robe, got into the closet, shut the door, and lay with my back against it so no one could come in. I sat there for the next hour, crying and crying. I felt like a failure as a wife, a mother, and as an employee. I started planning an escape route, how I could possibly run away.

At some point, I pulled myself together, got dressed, packed a bag, and stormed out of the house. On the way out, I screamed at David. I told him how awful he was and that he was screwing up our marriage and our child by failing to support me. I told him I'd packed a bag and was leaving, then drove away without a set destination in mind. I had no idea what I was doing and nowhere to go. I called my girlfriend Kerrie on a whim, and she let me come over to her house, where I proceeded to unload on her.

Meanwhile, David was calling and texting, and I knew he was in a panic, but for some time I couldn't bring myself to respond. I was up in Parker, and I eventually told him to meet me at the park by our old house. When he arrived, I was sitting on the swings, a disheveled mess. He came over and sat next to me, and we proceeded to fight through everything, pointing fingers, blaming one other, picking things apart. It was not a kind or loving conversation, and I still feel awful for what I did to him that day. After four years together, it was the first fight we'd ever had.

It felt like aliens had invaded my body. In retrospect, I can see that I wasn't *me* that day. I certainly didn't mean the things that I was saying. I found myself yelling at him for trivial things, like how long it took him to pick out juice when we were grocery shopping. I went on and on about how much I hated shopping with him, how he was so slow, reading all the labels before buying anything, evaluating multiple products before finally making a decision. The fact that he couldn't just grab some juice and put it in the cart was infuriating to me. I hated standing there in the aisles, watching him. As I went on and on, he just looked at me, crying, as I broke his heart.

We ended up walking away, agreeing to take some time to think and figure things out. Then, over the next few days, nothing budged. Things at work remained very stressful, and David and I couldn't manage to have a good conversation. Finally I called my doctor, told her what was going on, and asked for help. They wasted no time and told me to come in right away. When I did, they diagnosed me with postpartum depression.

At the time, I didn't even know what postpartum depression was. It doesn't happen right away—it typically creeps up four to six months *after* you have your baby. They immediately put me on medication and told me it could take up to a week to start working. But within an hour it felt like the clouds started to part. Everything just lifted off me. It felt like the invading aliens departed my body. I'd gone to Target to pick up the prescription, and I felt like the medicine started working as I was sitting in the parking lot. The weight of everything just lifted right off my shoulders.

Within an hour it felt like the clouds started to part. Everything just lifted off me.

As it did, reality started to set in. I realized how much of a monster I'd become and how much apologizing I had to do. I drove right home to my husband. The second I saw him, I started crying and apologizing profusely. He didn't understand mental health at that time either—even considering things like chemical imbalances was a new concept for him.

Next, I looked at my baby, who I'd been treating like a burden, an impediment, the cause of my lack of sleep. I'd been blaming my innocent child for getting in the way of my career and causing me stress. As I held him, my heart broke as I realized the full extent to which I'd been a terrible mom.

Then, through God's grace, my husband forgave me. That's what's so special about him—the extent to which he loves me and the extent of his faith. He trusts the Lord from the depths of his heart. In that moment, he could have done a hundred different things, but he just decided to take my apology sincerely, love me, and forgive me, which is exactly what I needed.

It was time for me to do something different with my life. There were so many repairs and decisions to make. I knew that what was going on at work wasn't sustainable *and* that I was about to get a six-figure-plus commission check. I'd been back at PayCo for almost three very successful years, sold millions, and brought on wonderful clients, but it was time to move on.

When I put in my notice, my manager asked me not to tell anyone, because they didn't want to ruffle any feathers. Then, when my time was finally up, I just quietly returned my laptop. Nobody called to do an exit interview, and I never got a call from my regional manager. My exit was as anticlimactic as can be—most of the people in the organization had no idea that I'd even left. That was fine. I had plenty of work to do.

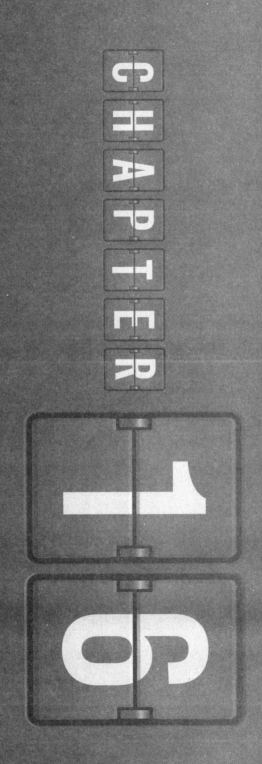

CHAPTER

16

CHAPTER 16

I wasn't quite ready to start my own company, but I knew I wanted to consult, and I knew I wanted to continue solving complex problems. I fell back on networking, and as I talked to people about sales training and consulting, one of my friends told me they had someone I needed to meet. He made an introduction to a very well-connected management consultant, who himself told me he had yet *another* person I needed to meet. "She's an author with an incredible sales training firm, and she's trying to find a successor. She wants to work side by side with someone for a couple of years, then enter into a management buyout."

That's exactly what I want, I thought. I'd never heard of her, her company, or her book, but when I started digging, everything felt aligned. She was very talented and accomplished, her book was incredible, and her brand was beautiful. After having a few conversations, I felt very comfortable with her, and vice versa.

She brought me on as a salesperson so I could prove myself before we started making real moves. She paid far less than I was making at PayCo, but that was okay, because I saw the bigger picture. I wanted to show her that I knew what I was doing, enter a management buyout, take over, and let her sail off into the sunset.

After I started, it took no time at all to realize that we were two visionary alpha females with very different visions for how to do things. While I was working for her, I started to have a lot of ideas. I'd go to her and say, "What if we did it like this?" In retrospect, I think that was exhausting for her. She still saw the company as hers, and her attitude was, *Do it my way or get outta here.* Though I loved what she did, our communication wasn't strong. I still proudly proclaimed to the world that I was associating myself with her and her company, and to this day, I have a lot of respect for her and her proven sales methodology.

But as time went on, I knew I couldn't spend two years doing things her way. We simply didn't agree, and that's okay. I was left with little choice but to say, "Okay, I'm out." At the

We simply didn't agree, and that's okay.

time, it kind of hurt, and I still feel bad about it—I owe her an apology for exiting abruptly but simply couldn't see an opportunity for us to work together over the long term. And in the end, I still did quite well for her—I'd sold a few hundred thousand dollars of sales training and consulting services in what felt like no time at all.

After leaving, I took a week to think long and hard. I didn't have a job lined up or even a good idea of what I wanted to do next. In that brief season where I wasn't working, I spent all day and night ideating and exploring. Rylie had long since moved to LA to pursue acting, but we were as close as ever. As before, I went to her for advice. I remember how scared I was about what to do next, and as always, she set me straight with a transformative pep talk. Rylie sent me one of Reese Witherspoon's famous speeches: "If you want something done, do it yourself."

Rylie understood my fears about becoming an entrepreneur better than anyone else. She'd been there as I tried to run my first company, and saw firsthand how unpredictable, expensive, and hard it was. Now the stakes seemed even higher because I had a family. When I was single and living by myself, I could make mistakes and go for broke. That was no longer an option. My family depended on my income, and I knew I couldn't mess up, because in November, I'd found out that I was pregnant.

I'd already fallen very deep into my faith through that season, partly as a way to move beyond my postpartum depression—once I got on medication, I dove straight back into my faith and the Word. I was listening to a lot of sermons as a way of searching for my life's purpose. *Who am I? What do I want to do? How can I honor God?*

At the same time, my friend Carolann had started a nonprofit, and the more we talked about it, the more it got me thinking about starting my own. I had the name *No Life Apart* in mind, both in the sense of "We all have one life to live" and of not having to separate one's Christian life from their work life. I wanted to let people know that you can live *one* life, *without* being a closeted Christian. On top of everything else, I was considering speaking, podcasting, writing, and beyond.

The night I was talking to Carolann, I suddenly started to feel a pain in my abdomen, and before I knew it, I had to run to the bathroom to miscarry. I couldn't believe it—I was only six weeks along and thought we were about to start an entirely new era. As my thoughts settled, I took comfort in realizing that God must've had something else in store for me.

Soon thereafter, I wound up at yet another networking event and ran into Trevor, an old CEO contact from when I'd worked at EMC. When he told me he was having trouble with one of his salespeople,

I told him I'd be happy to help with training to get things on track. That got me thinking: *What if I just start my own little sales training consulting company?*

And though I hadn't formed a company, built a website, or even printed business cards, I still had my reputation. Trevor knew I was the real deal. His company allowed me to do a bit of beta testing on my sales training and coaching, and that allowed me to calibrate how exactly to build out packages for customers around those services. When I came to them with a quote, their response was, "Great, let's do it." All of a sudden, I officially had my first client.

At that point I had to go over the noncompete agreement I'd signed with the lady I'd been working with, where I ultimately hadn't done a very good job. My own training methodology was too close for her comfort, and she sent me a cease-and-desist letter—which was the right thing to do! I was only thirty-three and still growing. I got so excited and courageous about potentially starting my own company that it made me feel a little entitled, making this another opportunity for a public apology. Today, I'm thankful for that cease and desist, which was ultimately an opportunity for me to redirect.

As I refocused on figuring out how to become a sales training consultant, I gravitated toward the name *Sales BQ*. BQ stands for *behavioral quotient* and is an adaptation of the behavior wheel: how you think triggers how you feel, how you feel fuels your behavior and your actions, and these collectively yield results, whether positive or negative. The core idea is that *it's all a cycle*—over and over, your results influence how you think, and the process starts all over again. I was and still am very passionate about all this. The behavior component is the missing ingredient in so much of sales—you can *learn* about sales, and you can have emotional intelligence, but BQ goes back to actually *doing the work*, and there are so many salespeople who are all talk and no action. More and more, I wanted to become a thought leader in that space, because I had—and still have—so much to say about this.

Once I had some momentum, things kept moving fast. I fell into a conversation on LinkedIn with another former payroll client with a sales problem, kicked off a part-time contract with them, and promptly started revamping *their* sales department. Then I had yet *another* chat with a former client from the Butterfly Creative days that led to a third client engagement.

In a matter of *weeks*, I'd landed my first three clients. My plan was to become a fractional VP of sales for each of them, build what I was offering into a more formal program, and eventually announce it to the market. It didn't take long—by January 2018, I'd formally incorporated, announced that I was officially launching a company, and made my first LinkedIn post. I was officially in business.

It was a proud moment—I was finally stepping back out as an entrepreneur. I have to give another huge shout-out to my husband here. I'd originally come to him to say, "The entrepreneur inside of me is ready to do this,"

> **It was a proud moment—I was finally stepping back out as an entrepreneur.**

and all he said was, "Great. Do it. Why not?" All along, he was so supportive. He never told me no. He always simply told me to *do what I needed to do*. He allowed me total freedom, never got concerned with what we had in savings, and never put any pressure on me whatsoever.

Once again, I went all in, and this time around, it wasn't my first rodeo—I had a clear business model and paying clients right out of the gate. As always, I kept networking. When I announced that I'd started the company, one of my connections reached out and asked if I wanted to be a speaker at the South Metro Denver Chamber. *Of course.*

I put together a talk, "Two Shockingly Simple Secrets to Unlocking High Growth Sales," and it launched me onto the speaking circuit. It became my signature keynote, and I went on to deliver it at least fifteen times that year. That first was in February—the CEO of a marketing company came right up to me after my keynote to say, "We need what you do." Then it hit me: *When I speak, I get a client. It's so simple.*

My next thought was, *I already have three clients. How am I going to take on a fourth?* My schedule was already quite full, but I took them on anyway. Before long, I was putting in anywhere from sixty to eighty hours a week, and the focus of my networking shifted from finding clients to finding contractors.

As the work began to snowball, Rylie and I decided that she needed to become my first contractor. She became my right hand, my confidante, and employee number one, all from Los Angeles, and helped with marketing, social media, and all the administrative tasks I could throw her way.

By February, I had two more contractors: Rob, a fractional VP of sales, and Steve, who helped with recruiting and sales training. I was so excited to have them onboard and to be building out a team in general. In no time we landed our fifth, sixth, seventh, and eighth clients. By spring, we were bursting at the seams, and I had to bring on yet another contractor from PayCo to help with sales training.

By June we had eleven clients, and things were getting real. All of a sudden, I had a full-speed-ahead company on my hands, and my speaking calendar showed no signs of slowing. As our monthly revenue was approaching $40,000, I brought two more people on the team. Even now, thinking about that time almost makes me dizzy: I'd started the company almost on a whim, beta tested with a few clients in the fall, announced the business's existence around the new year, and was looking at a half-a-million-dollar run rate by the summer. I was truly shocked. *How did this happen?*

Over three years running my first company, I'd never gotten anywhere close to what we'd been able to accomplish in those first five months. I can provide no other answer than the Lord having a hand in my business and building it with me. I felt like I was following the path I was meant to be on, and it was such an exciting journey. We were doing really great work for our clients, and they were seeing great results in turn.

By the time fall rolled around, we were doing well over $60,000 per month. Every time I did another speaking engagement, we brought on two to three new clients, and bigger ones were continually entering the pipeline. Meanwhile, we didn't even have an office, I wasn't paying for software to run the business, and we still had zero overhead except paying contractors. With only a dinky little website, I'd wound up with a profitable business from day one.

I knew business would continue to explode and that I'd need to convert some of my contractors into real-deal, full-time employees. That scared me a bit—when you convert people to employees, it introduces new costs and creates overhead. Regardless of whether you have revenue coming in or out, you have to pay your people. But I knew I had to put on my big-girl pants, so I started converting everybody to real employees.

The more I traveled for speaking engagements in 2018, the more my family life became a blur. Though it felt like we'd become a great team, David was running the show at home. He focused on ensuring that Beckham was where he needed to be, and GG was helping out a lot too. While I'm sure plenty of notable, wonderful things happened with my family during that time, a lot of it is foggy to me to this day.

I'd leave the house early, work late, and grind through the weekends. I was traveling almost every week, and when I *was* "around," I was so consumed by work that it probably didn't really feel like it to my family. The bottom line is that I wasn't fully present at home in my business's early days. I'm still proud of myself for what we accomplished, but I deeply regret failing to balance the professional success with quality time with my family.

What's worse is that I was initially oblivious to the fact that I was neglecting them at all—I still had the mindset that grinding at all costs was what I was *supposed* to do. I'd started a company from scratch, and I wanted it to be successful, period. I poured everything into it that I possibly could, and we ultimately turned it into something worth celebrating. In that first year, we closed out with our revenue at around a half a million—extraordinary for a first-year company. Then, as if to test my mettle, just as things were getting real, our profits dropped almost $9,000 before slowly rising again. Though I didn't fully realize it at the time, I'd bolted myself to a roller coaster.

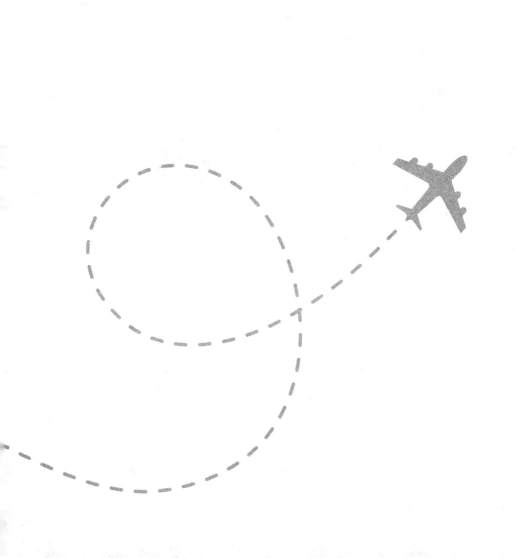

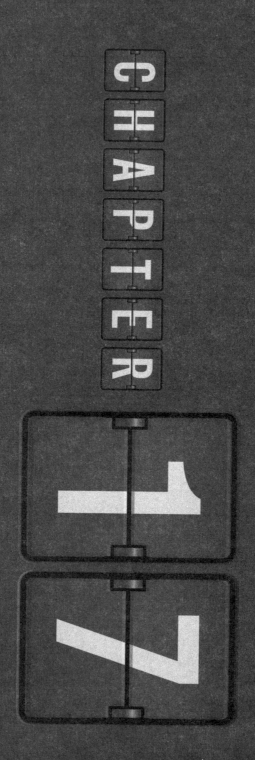

CHAPTER

17

CHAPTER 17

Over the next year, we turned into a real company. Early in the new year, as we were gaining momentum, I was having lunch with my friend and colleague, Steve, one of my sales trainers—older than me, mature, always full of good counsel on growing the business. I was telling him, "I'm really serious about growing the company. I think we need to get an office and do this for real."

This surprised him. "We've only been in business a year. You need to be really cautious about getting an office—it could really hurt us financially. If the business goes under, you'll be stuck with a three-year lease and a personal guarantee. How well are we *actually* doing?"

"Well, I think we're going to close the year around $450,000." Before I could continue any further, the look on his face told me everything I needed. He had no idea that we'd done that well in our first year. When I told him our run

When I told him our run rate was over $50,000 a month, he couldn't believe it.

rate was over $50,000 a month, he couldn't believe it. Until then, I hadn't really thought about our success at that level—I knew we were doing good work, but when I saw Steve so blown away by our growth, I knew we were onto something.

Soon thereafter, I had an amazing opportunity to present my keynote in front of two hundred CEOs. By the time I'd finished, the audience was absolutely stunned. It wasn't until I'd stepped off stage that I learned that *the entire audience* was composed of payroll CEOs, presidents, and owners. Just like that, our business practically doubled overnight. By the end of January, we were doing $90,000 a month in revenue, and by February, we'd crossed $100,000 in monthly revenue.

We ended up moving into that new office, and a lot of it came down to wanting to create a sales training center—I wanted to set up a trendy, cutting-edge space where we could hold sales trainings. I rented an inexpensive two-story warehouse, very industrial, with big garage doors. Jeff, the husband of one of my employees, is a contractor and family friend of David's from way back, and he came in to spice up the place. He was also a facilities manager at Ikea, so hiring him came with a great discount.

All in all, it was such a beautiful experience, but we had some difficulties leading up to our ribbon-cutting event. People always say to avoid hiring friends or family, and back in 2018 I'd brought on Jeff's wife, Kristina, to help with sales training. As the demands on the business grew on the recruiting side, she started to act more like a full-time recruiter. It wasn't really what I'd hired her for, but she was very good at it—she worked very hard and showed me a lot of loyalty—after all, we were family friends.

The business was growing faster than our ability to manage it, and I put a lot of pressure and expectations on her, especially in opening up our new office—far beyond what she'd originally signed up for. She was supposed to be our director of training and recruiting, and after some time I was asking her to order and assemble furniture, manage the remodel process, and generally direct all the operations and logistics of moving into our new space.

I only realized retrospectively how unfair that all was to her—she was so competent that it made it easy to dump things on her. As I was learning the ropes of being the young CEO of a legit company, I pushed her well beyond her max, which naturally made her more and more unhappy. When she started failing to pull through on things I really needed her to do, I became frustrated and didn't deal with it well at all.

Especially after reading books about this, now I recognize that I simply wasn't yet mature enough to be a great CEO. I'd converted this hustle-and-grind mentality from my sales years and tried to make everyone work like me. My capacity for grinding is just greater than the average person. I'd built a business that ran at *my* speed, which feels unrealistically fast to most people.

In the business's early days, I unconsciously expected everyone around me to operate at that same level. In the process, people disappointed me as I burned them out left and right. My unrealistic expectations led me to attempt to pick up the extra slack, which turned into many consecutive hundred-hour weeks. Fundamentally, I didn't know what I was doing, so I spent a lot of time running around like a chicken with my head cut off. I still had so much ego and arrogance and blamed others for not being "good enough." It took at least another year to truly appreciate that my capacity for urgency and risk-taking was around double of the average person on my team. All the while, the business continued to grow faster than my (and our) ability to handle it. Every time I spoke, it was like clockwork: *boom*, new clients.

By the time our ribbon-cutting ceremony rolled around in February, I was stressed beyond belief. I'd invited hundreds of people and wanted everything to go smoothly, because I could feel the eyes of the business community on us. I was still in the early stages of becoming a Christian and healing from my past wounds and was drawn to that old glow of success and recognition. There were still holes inside of me, and again I was attempting to fill them through success and recognition.

Having that grand opening ribbon-cutting ceremony was a way to prove to people, and to myself, that I was worth something, that I was a real CEO, that I was talented, that I was *special*. And the party *was* huge—a couple hundred people rolled through. We got a lot of press on social media, took a lot of great photos, and used the imagery for weeks afterward to keep the PR buzz alive, which attracted even *more* business.

Meanwhile, I was acting like a hard-ass, burning my people out and neglecting my family by grinding until I passed out. As David ran the show at home, I was managing somewhere between five to seven of my own clients on any given day on top of my five- to seven-person team.

No part of my experience had driven home the need for infrastructure, checklists, systems for onboarding and training.

I'd *started* building out manuals and templates to document processes and expedite training people, but it was all very haphazard. I'm not a manager by trade, and I don't really like infrastructure and detail work. By nature, I'm more of a wing-it kind of gal, so many things in those early days were a little ... *undefined*, if you will. We had no infrastructure or technology for communication, no real policies, no statements of purpose, no standardized way of operating. Everyone was just creating work from scratch, and there was no true rhyme or reason for doing anything.

At the time I thought, *Well, I don't preplan for all kinds of things, but we're still killing it.* I usually just winged it and won. No part of my experience had driven home the need for infrastructure, checklists, systems for onboarding and training, and people in place to advise me on how to best do my job. I'd always been able to figure everything out so fast, and I initially built a company where the expectation was for everyone to do the same.

I was also never trained on how to hire people. I didn't know how to screen or how to ask the right questions in interviews, which led to bringing on talent that wasn't necessarily a great fit for the company. When those people didn't thrive in their positions, I had to overcompensate and do their work for them. Then, when that started to spiral out of control, I became very quick to let people go, which is one of the hardest things to do as a CEO—or at least it was for me.

All the while, I was still traveling nearly every week to make keynotes. I can't count the times I flew to LA and back on the same day: out at dawn, back at nine or ten at night, working a full day in between, burning the candle at both ends. But looking back, I have to admit it: I loved it, because I thrive in chaos. For people who grew up in chaos, it all feels normal, and we *work* to recreate the chaos of childhood later in life, because it's what's comfortable. Yes, I was tired; yes, I was working hard; and yes, there was stress and pressure, but that all became my normal. I'd built, and was attempting to scale, a company that was chaotic to its core.

Nevertheless, we were using a sales benchmarking assessment tool to boil sales training down to a science: analyzing our clients' sales teams, identifying their areas of weakness, and building effective plans to resolve them. In the early stages of the business, the tools we were using provided some semblance of a framework for what we did, and it was beautiful. We'd sell those assessments and then tell our clients:

here are ninety-nine problems with your sales team, and here's how to fix each and every one.

A large industry-wide conference was coming up in Boston that April, and everyone who was using that sales benchmarking assessment tool was required to attend. Kristina was coming with me, and our relationship had steadily gotten rockier and rockier. It was so sad, but the lead-up to the ribbon cutting had driven a wedge between us, and I was already contemplating whether she should even be working for us. If I was going to let her go, I knew I'd at least have to wait until after the trip, because her work was central to our sales assessment—she knew the infrastructure and process inside and out: how it worked, how we sold it, how we delivered it.

We were supposed to be rooming together and traveling together—the whole kit and caboodle. We met up, parked her car at Ikea, and headed to the airport. As soon as she got into my car, I could see she was a mess. Her dog was deathly ill, and her entire family thought the dog was going to die. It had eaten something it shouldn't have, and its stomach and intestines were completely torn up. Looking back, I can see now that I was not only a bad boss but a bad person. I simply did not know how to extend her grace or empathy. I should have told her right away, *Do not come on this trip. Go home and be with your family. Take care of your dog.*

But I never did. We proceeded straight to the airport. Then, as we were sitting at the gate waiting to board, she got a call from her husband saying that the dog had passed away. This was yet another opportunity for me to say, *Get a taxi to your car and go home. I can handle this.* Yet again, I didn't. I was still acting like I was at PayCo, where you did your job and you succeeded at all costs. I simply didn't know any other way.

Meanwhile, there were so many difficult things in my own life that I wasn't tending to, because work always came first. I carried around these expectations: *Things happen, people get sick, dogs die. You still have to get your job done.* As we were traveling, I could tell she was trying to hold it together and be strong. She knew our relationship had become rocky and was probably already worried about keeping her job, because she was making great money, and I knew she passionately cared about doing a good job.

Unsurprisingly, the trip was difficult, and it made my own anxiety kick up. I was venting a lot to Kristina about all the stress and pressure on my plate and expressing a lot of frustration and disappointment in our people. I'm sure the environment I created for her was confusing and difficult to understand—a lot of the time, she clearly really didn't know how to respond, and I don't blame her. I deeply regret all this—my lack of professional maturity, my pride, my obsession with succeeding and winning at all costs. When we got back, the wedge between us continued to grow, and I knew it wasn't sustainable.

Meanwhile, Rylie had announced that she was leaving LA and moving back to Colorado. Right away I told her, "Great. You get a full-time job." She'd been working for me as a contractor and handling our marketing all along, and when she came back home, she recommended we add marketing consulting as a service for our clients, and she was willing to take it on. Half of them had no brand or marketing engine. She was still young but, as always, mature and knowledgeable beyond her years. My plan became to give half of Kristina's job to Rylie, then hire a full-time recruiter to fulfill the rest of Kristina's role.

When it came time to let Kristina go, I was a mess. I was losing sleep, breaking out, and feeling sick. I talked to David and GG about it, because she was *their* family friend, and I didn't want to cause an issue beyond the business. As always, David was my biggest cheer-leader, gave me a pep talk, and coached me through it, and even then, it was still so, so hard. I'm just not a confrontational person, period. I was unable to stand up to my mom for twenty-eight years, and then, when I finally did, all hell broke loose. That can't help but unconsciously swirl around in the back of your mind: *Confrontation is bad. Don't speak up. Don't stand up for yourself.*

Up to that point, I'd always managed to get through breakups while avoiding confrontation—even when I moved out of my ex-husband's house, we got the moving truck in secret, when I could've been strong and told him, *I want a divorce, and I'm leaving you because you're awful.* In most of my other bad relationships or jobs, I'd just cut and run. It's what I did at the IT cloud company: I knew their culture was toxic and that I had to get out, so I just locked my laptop in my cubicle, left the rest of my things on my desk, walked out, and sent in a resignation via email.

That approach had worked for me before, but it doesn't fly as a CEO. In those early days, I didn't know how to give employees feedback or how to hold them accountable. Instead, I'd stuff it all down and try to influence the environment around me to *indirectly* change people's behavior. When that inevitably didn't work, I'd either get frustrated and blow a gasket or talk behind someone's back and wait for the word to get back to them. Failing either of those things, sometimes I'd resort to putting so much pressure on people to perform that they'd burn out and quit, which, sadly, was my preference—I'd even *pray* for people to quit so I wouldn't have to go through the emotional turmoil of firing them.

But Kristina was not about to quit, and with Rylie coming on, I knew I had to muster the courage to go through with it myself. On the day it happened, I woke up panicked and nervous and somehow started feeling the courage to pull the trigger out of nowhere. I called David from my car for a quick pep talk, and he told me, "If you're feeling it, go and do it. Call me afterward. You're going to be okay. Just be kind and let her know what's not working."

I called her into my office, and it was one of the hardest conversations I've ever had. I told her that she wasn't meeting the requirements of the role and that I needed someone who could and that I was eliminating in-house recruiting. We processed her termination as a layoff, and she remained on payroll for some time to have a cushion. When she walked out, she hugged me and said that we were better friends than we were coworkers. All I could do was agree.

I started bawling hysterically from the rush of emotions, and the moment made me realize on a new level how much power and responsibility I'd taken on as CEO. I'd watched others in leadership positions before and acknowledged their power, but until that moment, I'd never necessarily considered *myself* as someone with power. Even though I had the CEO title, I had always just felt like a peer to my people. Up to that point, I'd never truly owned my authority. I'm not a chest pounder. I don't thrive on telling people what to do or being in charge—if anything, all of that frustrates me. I just wish people would take care of their own business, get things done, and do what they were hired to do.

Of course, I *do* like to work for myself and make my own decisions—working for other people was always difficult because I like to find better ways of doing things. And the bigger the company you work for, the less influence you have on changing the way things are done. Being a CEO gave me the freedom to do things how I wanted, but I didn't like everything that came with it. When I fired Kristina, the full weight of my power and responsibility hit me. I'd forever altered someone's life simply through the power of my words and actions. Doing that to her hurt me to the core, and from there I had to fundamentally rethink how I was leading.

This all led me to start working with a coach, Doug, on how to mature as a CEO and a leader. I originally met him in a networking group when I was still working for PayCo, when he'd offered a free session to anybody who wanted to try out his coaching. When we did our first session, I couldn't stand him—I thought he was arrogant and rude and felt like he spent the entire hour digging into me. Because I wasn't ready to open up, I felt very defensive and closed off, and we still laugh about it today.

It took some time to realize that he was really onto something and that I needed help. I came back later and apologized, fessed up to not having been very kind or open the first time around, and now he's been in my corner ever since. From the start, he helped me to start showing up differently as a leader.

It helped enormously that Rylie came on full time right when I needed her the most. I needed a friend and confidante, someone that I could trust fully. As usual, we were two peas in a pod. She's such a hard worker, so loyal, and so smart. And when she can't figure something out immediately, she keeps at it until she does. She's so resourceful and mature for her age, and at the time, she was just about to turn twenty-one.

With Rylie around, work became a lot more fun. I had a best friend in the business, and that made all the difference. She helped me tremendously with building infrastructure and processes *and* significantly elevated our brand and marketing engine. She was also entrepreneurial enough to see right away that we needed to integrate marketing into our service offering. We sat down and did a review of our clients, and when we started combing through the data, it was crystal clear: the clients with strong brands and marketing engines *dramatically* outperformed those who didn't.

Our core work at the time had been building sales departments for small businesses, often in teams of one to three or four. It *was* working, but half of the time, it was working about twice as well for those whose marketing was on point. Some of our clients still had terrible websites, no marketing collateral, no inbound leads, and weak Google rankings, and their sales teams bore the brunt of it. It was clear that we'd need to partner with a marketing firm or start offering marketing services ourselves.

We decided to adopt Rylie's plan and immediately put it to the test. She threw herself into auditing and research, managed the data, and crafted our plan of attack, all while handling a couple of clients on her own. At the same time, we tested various outside options, partnered with two marketing agencies to see how they could supplement our clients, *and* hired a fractional chief marketing officer (CMO)—she didn't come cheap, but it helped us to start building out our marketing engines.

In the end, both marketing agencies let us down—it was hard to juggle the competing timelines, processes, and pricing models, all while managing client expectations. Rylie came in second place, mostly because she was overloaded—on top of working long hours for us, she was also earning her college degree on the side. Rachel, our new fractional CMO, came out on top—she was absolutely brilliant and understood marketing at a far higher level than Rylie or me. She ultimately helped us build our marketing engine, and through her we became familiar with the term *revenue operations*, or RevOps, which is the combination of the operational workflow of marketing, sales, and customer success team members and the technology they use, like a CRM and marketing and sales automation tools.

Meanwhile, our VP of sales operations, Liz, did a lot of research on competing CRMs, and in the end, she narrowed it down to HubSpot. When Rachel concurred, it was on. I had coffee and a very open conversation with a HubSpot enterprise salesperson named Josh, and he taught me the basics of RevOps from the ground up. The more I learned, the more relevant it seemed to what we were doing. It became clear that we had a lot more to offer our clients than sales training, marketing, and branding —we had all the capacity in the world to be a fully fledged RevOps partner to our clients.

It became clear that we had a lot more to offer our clients than sales training, marketing, and branding.

As our service offerings expanded, we continued to grow like crazy. I was still doing a keynote or two per month, and on increasingly large stages. Our revenue grew: October, $170,000; December, $200,000. For the year 2019, we grew by $1.55 million total—we'd more than tripled in size from the prior year.

It didn't come without trial and challenge. I was still completely neglecting my husband and my son, and GG was picking up the slack in a way she shouldn't have had to. We were constantly managing my travel schedule, David's work schedule, and Beckham's day care and nanny. Even managing our family calendar felt like a constant battle. My son and I were not spending a lot of time together, and our bond suffered. I loved him so much, but I also saw him as a burden to my high-performing career, on a relentless path to succeeding as a start-up CEO and proving to everyone that I was worth something. For some reason, I was addicted to success and still felt that my worth came from other's opinions of me.

All the while, I was leaving the house at five thirty in the morning to beat traffic and was always the first one in the office. It didn't matter if we had a blizzard or if my son was sick—I was going in to that office. I was stubborn. I simply could *not* allow myself to fail. I was relentlessly obsessed with growth to an extent that was almost romantic—I was fully prepared to give everything I had to my business until I was depleted to nothing and had sacrificed everything in my personal life in exchange.

As a result, my son preferred his daddy over me, and rightfully so. I never had breakfast with Beckham, and he wouldn't want to sit next to me at dinner—then, as a result, we'd always end up fighting over the table. He never wanted me to brush his teeth, give him a bath, or put him down to sleep at night. I took this all personally, and would tell myself, *It's just a phase. he'll grow out of it.* Deep down, I took it so hard, because it felt like my son didn't love me, and it was all my fault because I wasn't there for him. But yet, I wasn't willing to sacrifice my addiction to my success and change my behavior.

At the same time, I'd joined a group for female CEOs, and we'd meet once or twice a month to talk and share our challenges and triumphs. I remember how prideful I was of what I'd built and would compare myself to the other women. Of course, comparison is a thief of joy and a waste of time and energy. No two lives or people are created equally, and everyone's callings are unique, because God has a unique purpose for each of us.

Nevertheless, I can remember feeling grateful when I felt ahead of the others and regretful when I felt behind. The competitor inside of me *had* to rise to the occasion and trump everyone else. I had to win, win, win, because that's what I thought life was about. This all feels awful to admit. It tastes like vinegar coming out of my mouth, because I love and am so grateful for those women, all of whom I respect so much. The world had a hold on me. It owned me, even as a Christian woman. I loved the Lord, but I was losing the battle of who owned my life to the enemy and to the world.

When I look back on this time in my life, I mostly want to apologize. I'm so sorry for my arrogance and my ego. Even as a saved Christian woman with Jesus in my heart and the Holy Spirit coursing through my veins, they were there all along. My intentions were good, and my heart for the Lord was pure, but the sin, temptation, hurt, and trauma that I continue to heal from was making me show up as somebody I'm not, which I regret. I was and still am a broken sinner.

And through it all, the success kept coming. We started winning awards. I was named a top-fifty keynote speaker. We won an award for the fastest-growing sales training firm, and I still have that trophy up on my bookshelf. We appeared in top-one-hundred lists. I was featured in *Women of Denver* magazine—you name it. And despite the awards and recognition, I still had a fundamental emptiness on the inside. None of it was enough.

By the beginning of October, we hit $1 million in a single year, and threw a million-dollar party to celebrate. I was so proud of what we'd accomplished. We bought three-foot mylar balloons for each number in one million, rented out a winery, and had a chef come in to cook a delicious meal, and we partied until we could party no longer. It was one heck of a celebration, and I had the time of my life. To this day, I'm so grateful for the people that were there with me that night.

So many wonderful people showed me grace when I could have treated them better.

Go hug, or at least high-five, a start-up employee. These people *choose* to work in chaotic, unstructured, fast-paced environments, where things pivot on the daily. To any of the people who were with me that may be reading this book, I want to say a special thank-you—thank you for standing by my side and being part of my journey, despite my short fuse and unrealistic expectations. So many wonderful people showed me grace when I could have treated them better. Instead, so often, I burned them out. I apologize to everyone for whom I created anything less than a great experience—I learned so much in those early days and am so grateful for the time and the energy that everyone put forth.

After the party, we could not stop growing: $170,000 in October, $191,000 in November, $215,000 in December. That December, we had another company holiday party in a private room at Elway's Steakhouse, and I still fondly remember looking around the table at everyone there. We'd welcomed a couple of new employees, and everyone brought their significant others. David was next to me, toasting with a glass of wine, and I was so thrilled, grateful, and humbled to realize that this was *my* life and that I'd really built something. Apparently, all my hard work had finally paid off.

At the same time, I was exhausted, and there was no light at the end of the tunnel. The growth just kept coming. As we approached $2 million in revenue, I was in disbelief. We had more business than we knew what to do with, and I couldn't hire people fast enough. My phone was never off, and all the while I knew I wasn't taking care of myself. I could feel that my days were increasingly numbered from a health standpoint, but I didn't know how to slow the train down—it was going a hundred miles an hour and laying the tracks as we went.

I tried to take some time off between Christmas and New Year's. I wanted to be at home, unplug, and be quiet, but it wasn't to be. Rachel, our fractional CMO, was working around the clock, and I could feel in my bones that we were about to have a breakthrough. Throughout that week I was supposed to be off and decompressing at home but spent most of my time back home working. I had a feel for what the market wanted and knew that we were not only going to be able to significantly increase our average revenue per client but that our clients' results were going to dramatically improve.

I remember hosting an event for our women's CEO group around that time, and as we went around sharing what was going on in our lives and businesses, I cried tears of joy. I finally felt like I'd *done it*—that I was *somebody*, was *something*. I'd scaled a company to $1.5 million in less than two years—all this in a world where less than 1 percent of female-owned businesses scale past $1 million. I was absolutely beside myself with pride. But the joke was on me, because I was about to eat the biggest serving of humble pie of my life.

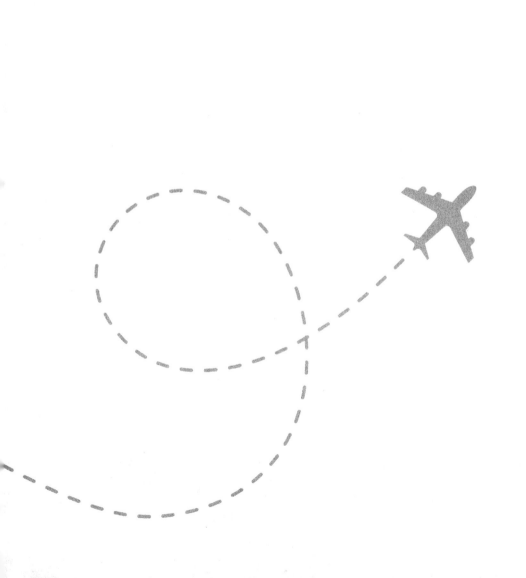

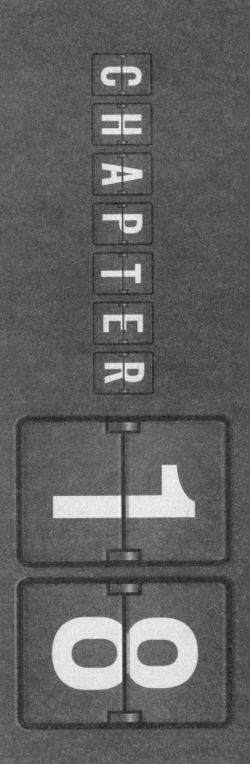

CHAPTER

18

CHAPTER 18

I continued flying around, doing keynotes and trainings. We started 2020 strong, with so much business in the pipeline. We were about to put a shiny new bow on our new service offering and were already testing it with a new client that we'd brought on in December. Everything was going extremely well. Then, in February, people started talking about this thing called the coronavirus.

I remember wondering, *Is this a thing? Is this not a thing? Should we be panicking? Should we not be panicking?* Like everyone else, I had my eye on it, but it seemed like a wait-and-see. Meanwhile, as the media had a field day and caused panic, the president got up and said the opposite: *The whole thing will all be over soon.*

At work, I couldn't help but notice that our pipeline was slowing down. We'd had $1 million in the pipeline and typically closed around half of it. More and more, people seemed to be stalling. Nevertheless, we launched our new service offering in early March, contracted with new VPs of sales and marketing, and continued to hire new team members. Our heads of marketing were brilliant, and our VPs of sales had more than doubled our average revenue per client.

All the while, I was riding the high of all highs, traveling every week, scaling, growing, hiring. Accolades, awards, press. Winning,

winning, winning. Then, of course, everything shut down. Practically overnight, one client after another started canceling—we lost eleven in three days. *I'm so sorry, we can't pay.* Our revenue dropped from $210,000 a month to $130,000.

I descended into sheer panic. I got on the line with my women's CEO group fully hysterical, grieving from the pit of my stomach. I felt the worst sense of failure I'd ever felt. I'd gone from feeling like the best CEO to the worst. The way things were going, I didn't think I'd even have a business for long. When all but one of the deals in our pipeline disappeared, I thought I was staring the end right in the face. Everything I'd worked and sacrificed so hard for came crashing down—two and a half years of blood, sweat, and tears gone in an instant.

When I got off that call, I walked out into our living room. My son was sitting on the floor, playing with his wooden trains. At that point, Mommy wasn't allowed to touch his trains—only Daddy was. Mommy wasn't allowed to do a lot of things, because Mommy *didn't have a relationship with her son.* David, meanwhile, was sitting on the couch watching TV.

The light from the television was illuminating Beckham's face. In that moment, I realized that I didn't recognize my own son. He'd grown up before my eyes, and I hadn't been there to see it. I sat down next to him, devastated, and just started crying. I looked over at my husband—this man whom I'd completely neglected for two and a half years. My better half. The man I'd prayed for. My gift from God, who had waited to bless me until I was ready and right with him, whom I'd taken for granted as he ran our house and raised our son.

As I sat there on the floor, I began to hate myself. After everything I'd worked so hard for had vanished in a matter of three days, I realized I'd made a very bad choice in obsessing over it instead of the gifts that God had given me: my husband, my son, and GG. Gradually, I began to feel sick and grateful in equal measure, because miraculously, against all odds, *they were still there.*

I hadn't lost them. I was already on my knees, sniffling and crying from the pit of my stomach, and I just prayed for God *to take it all away.* All of it. *Please, take my whole business. Take care of my employees, make sure they're okay, and then take the whole thing from me.* I repented from my sin, from neglecting my family, for worshipping success. I prayed for God to forgive me, and surrendered my career to him. I would rather pursue something—*anything*—else than continue trying in vain to prove to the world that I was worth something.

It was so hard for me to sleep that night. I was still sick to my stomach, hating myself for what I'd done. Then, when I woke up the next morning, there was a new peace inside of me. I felt that the Lord had forgiven me, was holding my hand, and was ready to instruct me in rebuilding my life—this time with him by my side.

That Sunday, my pastor did a sermon series called Unshakeable and spoke about the Passion Translation of Matthew 7:24–27:

> Everyone who hears my teaching and applies it to his life can be compared to a wise man who built his house on an unshakable foundation. When the rains fell and the flood came, with fierce winds beating upon his house, it stood firm because of its strong foundation. But everyone who hears my teaching and does not apply it to his life can be compared to a foolish man who built his house on sand. When it rained and rained and the flood came, with wind and waves beating upon his house, it collapsed and was swept away.

It felt like God was speaking directly to me. God gave me the gift of entrepreneurship, the gift of fearlessness, the gift of risk tolerance, high urgency, and high capacity. He knew my heart. My heart was in serving our clients, but my priorities were out of order. I felt the Lord telling me that he was *not* going to take my company from me and that we would rebuild it—together.

The business continued falling apart, but now I had peace inside of me. I started cutting expenses. I called our landlord and negotiated a cash payout to get out of our lease early. I looked at every expense I owed anyone and just started writing checks. As one client after another called to say they couldn't pay for our services, my moral compass sprang to attention. All at once, I decided that I was not going to be like the others.

There was no integrity in cutting and running.

There was no integrity in cutting and running. It wasn't ethical. I refused to do it to others, because I knew how hard it had been on *me*. Somehow, I believed that God was going to provide. I didn't even need to look at the balance in our bank account, because God was in charge, and I knew he was going to provide. I looked at every bill and every invoice for every vendor, and I paid them all. One after another, I wrote checks, put them in the mail, and didn't even look at the account balance. I could just *feel* God guiding me.

Next, I called a meeting with my team. I told them that although the going was tough, I was going to do everything in my power to preserve the people we had. In the end, I only had to let one under-performing team member go. As always, I struggled with having to terminate someone, and again, I processed it as a layoff so he could get unemployment. He was young, freshly married with no kids, and very talented and got another job quickly.

By that point, we were down to six employees, eight brave clients, and that last one in the pipeline. I went to them and asked how they'd like to proceed. They told me, "Well, we applied for a Small Business Administration loan, and it was just approved. We'd like to pay for your services in full." The man proceeded to write a big fat check for his entire six-month contract, which I was able to deposit into our bank account, and it covered almost all the expenses. We paid every vendor, and we got out of our lease. That, ladies and gentlemen, is how God works.

Our accounting and payroll firm helped us apply for a Paycheck Protection Program (PPP) loan, and that was the next miracle that ultimately saved us. The funds were deposited in April, and when they hit, I breathed a huge sigh of relief. God had taken away all the stress and worry. Our bank account had been perilously low, and now we had room to breathe. Within thirty days, everything had turned around.

We continued downsizing and cutting overhead. Everyone worked from home. I called for nine-to-four workdays. Even more importantly, all my flights were canceled—every trip, keynote, and speaking engagement. After losing twelve clients and a team member, I had far less extra work to do. For the first time in two and a half years, I was at home and unburdened.

The first thing I did was sleep. I slept like I hadn't slept in two and a half years. I stopped setting an alarm in the morning and became a mom and a wife again. The joy of the Lord was so present in our home. For the first time, my son let me make him breakfast, and we ate together every morning. I was suddenly allowed to play with his trains, allowed to read to him, allowed to do bath time with him, allowed to lie with him in bed at night as he fell asleep.

More and more, we started to rebuild our relationship. My husband and I rekindled the flame in our marriage. I apologized to him a thousand times, but the words can only go so far. He had to see me show up differently. I had to put down the phone and close my laptop at night and on the weekends so I could be present with him.

Despite the enormous pain it caused so many people, I'm so grateful for the pandemic—through it, God gave my family back to me. He hit a giant reset button in my life, and that allowed me to start taking care of myself again. I healed internally, became more whole spiritually, and started sleeping regularly, and my depression and anxiety abated. I dove deep into my faith and my home life, rebuilt my marriage, and cemented my motherhood, all on a solid rock with Jesus.

Miraculously, our business did $2.2 million in revenue—I made more money than I'd ever made, *and* I was happy and healthy. The shutdown went on for eight weeks in Denver before the state opened up at 50 percent capacity. Practically speaking, that meant that 50 percent of the workforce was allowed to work on rotating shifts.

We found a month-to-month coworking space at the end of May with cute little two-person offices, so Rylie, Liz, Rachel, a few others, and I moved right in. I loved going to that office—it felt like the sun had pierced the clouds. Life was so good. We were working hard, successful, and happy, and never forgot to take time for our families, our marriages, our friends, and our significant others. As always, I especially loved working with Rylie. She's my soul sister and brought so much joy into my life every day. For a long time, with no speaking engagements or conferences on my calendar, we were able to really focus on our brand and marketing.

By fall of that year, the market started to do virtual events, so I got to do virtual keynotes, which was exciting. Things continued to roll off my back. I was still all in, but nothing stressed me out. On top of the PPP loan, we also received the employee-retention tax credits, which helped tremendously. A lot of industries were forever scarred, but several businesses were fortunate enough to rebound, and we were one of them.

My heart was so pure during that season, so tight in my walk with the Lord. I vowed to never become a workaholic again, to never neglect my family again, to stay focused on remaining mentally well and healthy. I vowed to keep the business at its current size. I vowed to do remarkable work. I love Colossians 3:23: "Whatever you do, do it for the Lord." In other words, whatever you do for work, do it for the Lord—*not* for men. That's where your inheritance comes from.

When you consider eternal consequences, pleasing people and the world only goes so far. When we die, everything dies with us. But there's a life after this one. There's eternal life in heaven, and there will be consequences if we don't serve the Lord here on the earth. If I'm only serving man, then I'm destined to go through the wide gate, straight to hell—and during the pandemic, I chose to go through the narrow gate.

Back at home, we were starting to see tractors moving dirt around on the hill where we had originally wanted to build our dream house. The sight gave us mixed feelings—we were initially more distraught than anything, because those rolling virgin hills and the hundred-year-old pine trees on top of them were our magnificent view, the main thing that made our property incredible.

Meanwhile, I'd fallen in love with HGTV fixer-upper and house-flipping shows to the point of obsession. I was especially taken with the farmhouse style and had started making changes around our current house to reflect that. When a farmhouse model home started going up on the hill, we fell in love and had our real estate agent make sure we were first in line on opening day. Unfortunately, we couldn't match the house we wanted with the lots they had available.

I kept Zillow surfing, just like so many others during the pandemic—we'd fallen in love with our house, but I had an itch for a new one that just wouldn't quit. I have a very obsessive personality, one that I've prayed for God to take away, because it usually doesn't lead anywhere good. I think the only thing God wants us obsessing over is him—in the end, he's the only thing worth chasing after.

As our business continued to rebound from the COVID-19 pandemic, we came across a house from the 1950s on an amazing thirty-five-acre farm property. It needed a *lot* of work—I instantly thought, *Wow, my days of becoming Joanna Gaines have finally come.* She had become my lockdown idol, and I *still* love her. But the problem with idols—and obsessing over things besides Jesus in general—is that I was never meant to be Joanna. *Joanna* was meant to be Joanna. I'm not meant for living on a farm, picking up a hammer and nails, and tackling a home-renovation project, but at the time my line of thought was, *If she can do it, so can I.*

The house needed to be gutted and renovated completely—a lot of people would've probably just knocked the whole thing down. The appeal was more about the lush green fields it was surrounded by and the amazing views—to this day, it's one of the most stunning properties I've ever seen. It became available Memorial Day weekend and was listed at $950,000—take it or leave it.

Somehow, I convinced David that we should buy it, which is yet another indication of how much he loves me. He didn't want to live there, or on a farm in general. He didn't want to deal with an old decrepit property or its falling-down barn. Yet he could see how excited I was, so like always, he just supported me.

I was being very selfish at the time—I'd just rebuilt my relationship with my son and my husband *and* my company. At the time, everything felt so good. When there's no chaos in my life and when things start to get too easy, I tend to manufacture chaos. It's another common trait of people who grew up in chaos—when things get a little too calm, we can't be comfortable, because chaos is what we're accustomed to.

We bought the house, and I drew up a three-month plan to renovate it. Then, as we went under contract and started to list our old house, I had a wicked panic attack. All of a sudden, it felt like the Lord was saying, *Mary, you're making a big mistake. Just keep the house you have.*

Meanwhile, our real estate agent sent over a woman to stage the house for the sale. She walked through each room while conducting her audit and told us exactly what we needed to do to make it salable. My house is filled with scripture—there's some kind of scripture in each and every room, almost on every wall. When she told us that every "religious artifact" needed to be taken down, it pierced me and crippled my heart. God is the only reason we had our first house to begin with, or could even consider buying a $950,000 farm property.

At the same time, I'm not an idiot—I know that in order to sell real estate, you need to neutralize your home—even family pictures need to come down—but I couldn't help but want to kick that lady right out of my house. By the time she left, I was done. I could just feel the conviction of the Holy Spirit inside of me, telling me, *Do* not *sell your house.*

From there I went straight into a tailspin and another panic attack. It felt like God's hands were almost shaking me awake, letting me know that what I'd been envisioning was not what he had in store for us. I opened up to David. "I don't feel comfortable selling our house. We need to figure out how to buy the farm without selling this one, but I have no idea how to make that happen financially."

"Well, why don't we just cash in some stock and use that toward the down payment?"

David's very frugal and very responsible. He'd been planning financially for years and had several hundred thousand dollars in stock sitting around in his retirement account. Meanwhile, Apple's stock had risen dramatically, so we sold some of that, and I took a draw out of the company toward our construction budget. We managed to negotiate down a bit on the property, then found a contractor.

I felt so grateful, but it only lasted for a moment—most who lived through the pandemic will remember how badly the construction industry got slammed with shortages. All at once, everybody wanted to build. Within thirty days of starting the project, our contractor's estimate more than doubled. I started to get nervous about irresponsibly overextending ourselves yet again.

After thinking long and hard about it, again, I went back to David.

"What if we just sold the farmhouse?"

As soon as the words came out of my mouth, he came to life. He lit up and looked at me with the biggest, most energetic smile, then agreed wholeheartedly. He'd just driven through the neighborhood behind our own, where he'd found a lot he really liked. When he brought me to see it the next day, I could feel the Lord's blessing all over it. It was *right* by the train tracks.

I realized all at once: any big family decision should be exactly that—a *family* decision. That farmhouse had been completely a *Mary* decision—it wasn't near the train tracks that were so important to my son and husband. There were already trains all over our house, and every time a train came by on the north- or southbound tracks, David and Beckham rushed to the window to watch it go by. My son has done this since he could walk, and David's been doing it about as long himself.

That farmhouse was tucked away behind the hills where you couldn't see the trains, and I felt like I'd selfishly taken something special from them by trying to move us away, and it broke my heart to realize that. I'd wanted that farm selfishly, without considering these two very important guys in my life.

As all this was happening, we became friends with one of my son's friend's parents at a birthday we threw him in the park. His friend's dad, Tony, was always talking about how he grew up on a farm in Georgia, how much they loved the country, and how they'd been looking for a farm property. When we told him about ours, he realized that he'd first gone to look at it by the time we'd put our initial offer in.

When we told him we were selling, he made us an offer right then and there. He and his wife work in the military, so they were eligible for a VA loan, but because VA loans can't be made on properties under construction, we financed the construction within our original budget, and then they moved right in. For all of this, I was so grateful. One, we'd made new friends. Two, they were able to use *us* to renovate *their* dream property—something they never would've been able to do otherwise. Everything worked out.

We stayed in our current home, with our eyes set on the lot that David loved. When it became available in September, we were able to go over and sign the paperwork, all on the five-year anniversary of Ron's death. Once the contract was signed, we went out there with the ceremonial shovel and took the picture of our new lot. What a blessing!

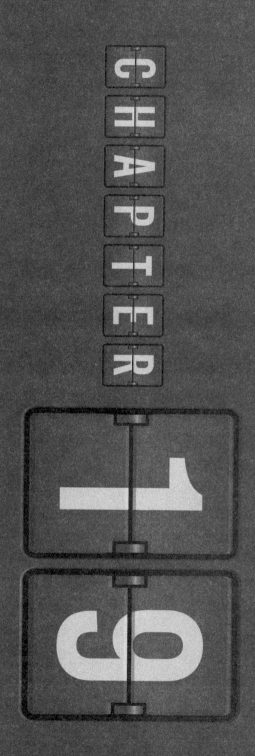

CHAPTER

19

CHAPTER 19

The economy started to pick up by the end of the summer of 2020, and our business went right up along with it. Once again, it was time to hire, grow, and add team members. I brought on a young man named Henry as a VP of marketing that August: young, hungry, passionate, multitalented, savvy in marketing, entrepreneurial, full of ideas, and extremely hardworking. From the second he came in the door, he had all kinds of ideas for how we could do things better.

At the time, I had zero aspirations for growth—I just ran the company and focused on keeping my life in balance. Whatever revenue we did, we did. I didn't have a budget or revenue goals. I wanted to be happy, and I was. I wanted our clients to be happy, and they were. I wanted my team to be happy, and they were too. I was focused on being a good wife, a good mom, and a good servant of the Lord. And I was.

Henry came in wanting to be a part of something special. More than anything, that meant scaling the company. His dream was to be the right hand for a CEO, help them scale, take a company to exit, and start his own company with the proceeds. These were not only beautiful aspirations but a very humble career path. It takes a lot of humility to come to someone and say, "My aspiration is to be *your* right hand." He wanted to gain the maturity, knowledge, and experience to be a successful entrepreneur and CEO—pretty admirable, I thought, for a twenty-seven-year-old.

I'd ceased being a hard-ass CEO and was growing into becoming a different kind of leader—empathetic and loving. I looked at my employees differently and replaced hustle and grind with empowerment and encouragement. I was deeply invested in our collective emotional well-being and did whatever I could to help our people grow and succeed. My pendulum had swung from the cutthroat, win-at-all-costs, get-it-done, no-excuses mentality in the entirely opposite direction, where I would've done anything for anyone. If someone asked me for something, I made it happen.

> I'd ceased being a hard-ass CEO and was growing into becoming a different kind of leader—empathetic and loving.

I was so happy with where we were that I hadn't put much thought into scaling the company, but Henry was a visionary, and it was contagious. My heart started to shift, and his energy was so infectious that he brought most of the team along with him. Like everyone, I took a liking to Henry and his ideas. My heart grew for him, and like everyone on the team, I wanted him to be successful. He was just an idea-generating machine and a complete natural at pointing out things that were broken or wrong and where we should have processes in place.

His dreams were bigger than mine, and I felt like I could be the person that was the primary catalyst for his success. Almost automatically, and without realizing it, that became my north star. I've always drawn energy from people telling me something's wrong or bad or that I can't do something. I can't help but get a thrill out of proving those people wrong.

A lot of Henry's ideas were irresistible, and they cumulatively shifted my focus to the things that were wrong with the company, instead of what was right. We were stable, profitable, and 100 percent successful with our clients, but slowly I started to take all that for granted. More and more, I said yes to a lot of Henry's ideas—building infrastructure, standardizing processes, solidifying the rationale for our pricing, packaging our offerings, all of which were great. Hats off to Henry for all of the above.

I'd certainly never aspired to scale to $5 million, $10 million, or $20 million and exit—I'd never even thought of an exit plan at all. I was just happy with the work I was doing and thought I was going to do it forever. Henry was completely up front and honest about his aspirations from day one, but I didn't really know what that truly meant until we got into the thick of our working relationship. The man is talented, kind, good, and empathetic. On top of that, boy, can he scale a company. I still have incredible admiration for him.

His vision was like a force of nature, and the more he articulated it, over and over, the more I would push it down. I remember having dinner with David and talking about it.

"I think we're going to try to grow the company, and to do that, we'll need to add a number of new roles."

David gave me a look. "Why can't you just keep it small? You're so happy. Why do you have to grow even more?"

"I don't know—I feel like the team really *wants* to grow, and we've already *been* growing year over year. I feel like everyone wants to continue that growth—millennials are all about purpose and meaning. Start-up culture is about being a part of something. There's a trade-off for working for a start-up—it's chaotic, and you have to hustle until you collapse, but there's the promise of a big payout at the end, right? You scale, you exit and make a bunch of money. Then you pat one another on the back, high-five over your beers in Mexico, reminisce about what you accomplished, take a break, recover, and then you go and do it all over again."

As Henry started growing in his role, many of our other people realized they had similar aspirations—he just brought that out in everyone. His vision had never been my vision, but it made me think, *I'd be a bad CEO if I didn't give my team what they want.* As always, it went back to wanting to be loved and, moreover, being the catalyst for my people to have extreme, life-changing success sounded like a lot of fun.

It *also* sounded like it would feed my ego, make me feel like I was worth something, and allow me to pat myself on the back and say, "Good job, Mary. You're great." It's just another example of how past trauma continues to inform how I operate today. It all springs from the belief that I'm never good enough.

All the work I'd done through 2020, healing and becoming whole, getting right with the Lord and with my family, and rebuilding my company—it all slowly started to go right out the window. By the end of 2020, we were hiring aggressively and in pursuit of Henry's vision.

When he arrived, we had only VP level-and-above employees— mostly VPs of sales and of marketing, each of whom worked with three clients apiece. They scaled their clients' companies for a year, then we'd graduate them and bring on a new client. Whenever we had more business than people to handle it, we'd add new team members. Simple.

Henry's vision was also quite simple. He wanted to forgo hiring more vice presidents, mostly because they're expensive. Instead, he wanted to hire two marketing execution specialists for every VP, which would theoretically free up the VPs to assume leadership roles, manage and oversee the marketing execution specialists, *and* take on more clients.

He modeled this all out, built an org chart, and presented a new business model. A large part of it was *not* graduating our clients after twelve months. If we had a larger marketing staff, we could maintain their contracts *after* we would have originally graduated them, convert them instead to marketing-only clients, and continue drawing recurring monthly revenue from their business. Henry essentially wanted to build a marketing agency inside of our consultancy.

Over and over again, I pushed it down: "No, no, no. I don't want to grow."

All the while, David could see the forest through the trees. "You finally just got your life back. Life is manageable. We're happy. Can we just not?"

But slowly, more and more I was countering with "Why not? Let's just give it a try. Worst-case scenario is it doesn't work, and we can just scale back to where we're at now."

As Henry, Rylie, and I focused on marketing and branding and moved away from merely being a sales training company, we all agreed that the name Sales BQ no longer quite described what we actually did. Clearly, we needed a rebrand. We went through a really exciting rebrand exercise, and of all people, David was the one who came up with our new name: House of Revenue.

I found this to be very Christ centered. It goes back to Matthew 7:24–27 all over again, about building your house upon a rock. At that point, I felt like we truly *had* rebuilt our house on a solid rock. The year 2020 had been such a powerful reset. By the following winter, we'd launched a whole new brand, most of which Rylie and Henry had built from scratch.

Meanwhile, I'd came back around to a revenue leader I knew named Paul. He'd come to us through a recruiter and declined our initial offer to work for one of our clients because he didn't think he was a good fit. As I was considering Henry's grand plan, I went back to Paul, told him I thought he was brilliant and that I wanted him to consider working for us, as a kind of hybrid sales and marketing VP.

The role of chief revenue officer (CRO) hasn't been around for long—they were originally glorified sales leaders, and now the title refers to people who are proficient throughout revenue: branding, marketing, sales, customer success, and revenue operations. Paul was the rare person who was solid in all of the above, and I thought he could be our first true CRO. He was young and hungry and had an awesome young family. He was out in LA, but the more we talked, the more he considered relocating his family to Denver.

He really was the best of the best. When he started, I didn't even have to onboard and train him—he just came on, put his head down, and hit the ground running. To this day, he's one of the best employees I've ever had. He just started scaling his three initial clients in a way I'd never seen, and his ROI was off the charts. I just knew I had to put him in a leadership position. I knew if he could get other people in the company to perform like he did, we'd win like no other.

Before long, I started to feel like I was losing control of my company.

And win we did—as expected, we grew like nobody's business through 2021. The more I said yes to Henry's vision, the more we expanded our team, took on new clients, and implemented our revamped, marketing-only contracts. After Paul, we hired another VP of marketing, and many more employees through the spring.

Then, before long, I started to feel like I was losing control of my company. It shouldn't have been a surprise—after all, the vision we were implementing was not mine, and because of that, I didn't have the drive or clarity to implement it. Unsurprisingly, my anxiety started kicking up in the worst way. Rylie, of course, was the first to feel it—she was the first to tell me, "This company is turning into something very different."

I loved our new name, but it bothered me that I didn't really *know* half the new team members we were bringing on. Up to that point, I'd known each and every team member intimately. When there are only five or six of you, that's only natural. Now we were growing so rapidly that I didn't have the time to even get to know our new people, who they were, or what they were about. At the same time, we were building middle management layers with no real training in place for them—there was still no infrastructure to manage people or create meaningful, instructive feedback loops.

By April, I'd entered into a very, very dark period. A new hire had resigned within their first ninety days, which had never happened, and we'd just brought on a client who'd specifically wanted to work with them. Word to the wise: that's a mistake—do not ever sell a client based on a specific team member, because when that team member leaves, that client won't want to be with you anymore.

I knew I needed to recruit and replace that employee, and in the process of doing so, I realized that I was already starting to overwork myself all over again. In just a few months, all my bad habits came roaring back: working late, working on the weekends, neglecting my family. I was traveling again for keynotes and conferences, and my workload was shooting through the roof.

Back at the office, I was conducting interview after interview, recruiting new people, building infrastructure, and writing job descriptions. Henry was helping with all this, but he still had his own clients to manage. To his credit, he was very effective and one of the best client-facing team members we had. But I still badly needed support, so I converted Henry to chief operating officer (COO) to save me from drowning in administrative work.

Soon our company quarterly meeting rolled around, and we flew in the whole team to spend a few days together, conducting meetings and learning sessions, listening to guest speakers, holding team-building events, and going out to have a good time. As it was all kicking off, I pulled up to the office, parked my car in the garage, and immediately started having a horrible panic attack. All of a sudden, I found myself shaking and crying. I turned on some of my Christian music to try to calm down. There I was, sitting in my car in the garage, singing along to Lauren Daigle's "Hold On to Me"—crying, hands stretched out to God, trying to shake myself out of it, praying for him to fix me—or at least fix how I was feeling.

I shook off the panic as best I could, went upstairs, and started helping Rylie set up for the meeting. I told her how emotionally distraught I was, hugged her, and started crying all over again. I told her that I felt like I'd completely lost control of the company, that I'd been neglecting my family again and was generally doing everything I said I wasn't going to do. She could have helped console me longer, but we had no choice but to start the meeting.

I looked around the room at the faces of all these strangers who apparently worked for my company. I'd watched recordings of their interviews and knew we'd hired them, but I didn't know who they truly were or who *I* was either. I remember thinking, *Is this what being a CEO is supposed to be like? This is just what happens when you get bigger? People that you've never even met just come and work for you?* It just felt *weird*. Standing in front of everyone, I could feel the panic attack coming back. I was numb almost to the point of a blackout for the subsequent two hours.

All the while, I was still trying to run the opening session. I went on autopilot and scarcely recognized the words coming out of my mouth. I just couldn't stop looking around thinking, *Who are you people? Whose company is this? What have I done?*

CHAPTER

20

CHAPTER 20

'd taken what God had given me, then said yes to someone else's vision, and it was my fault. I was the one who'd said yes. I take full responsibility and feel no ill will or hard feelings toward anyone involved at all. Henry is still one of the most talented people I've ever worked with, and I have no doubt that he'll go on to do absolutely remarkable things. I simply didn't know how to firmly say no. I wanted his dreams to come true and allowed myself to become the principal vehicle to make that happen.

At that point, there was also no stopping the train. I'd already promoted several people into leadership positions simply because I couldn't handle all the work on my own. In the meantime, we'd also decided to build an online revenue training academy. We were pouring thousands of hours across different team members into building and writing a curriculum, all while professionally filming and producing material.

Just before we kicked off that project, Rylie asked me to coffee one Saturday, and I knew what was coming. She told me it was time to spread her wings and go somewhere else. She told me that the company wasn't what it once was. I could only look back at her like, *No kidding*. Of course, losing Rylie was very difficult for me. I *needed* her. When she left, I knew I'd have to grow up and that I couldn't use her as a crutch anymore. Over and over, she'd helped talk me off the ledge, heard out my problems, and served as my on-call therapist.

Several people interviewed for her job, and I knew I'd found her replacement the second I met her. Her name was Sabrina, and she was a marketer in her midtwenties. What I didn't know at the time was that Sabrina was about to play a very, very big role in my life. She referred to herself as a Swiss Army knife of marketing, and it was true—she's truly multifaceted and had already worked in several different industries.

> **I knew I'd found her replacement the second I met her.**

Because she reported to Henry, I didn't get to work with her one on one much at first, but before long she was spearheading a refresh of our brand and was absolutely instrumental in taking it to the next level. She also went on to run the entire revenue academy project and, with a team of nine, built it beautifully from the ground up. Sabrina poured everything into the company. She worked nights and weekends, ran our brands, coordinated company events, and helped onboard new hires, all while remembering everyone's birthdays and anniversaries, for which she always somehow managed to find beautiful gifts. She was tremendously selfless and stepped up to the plate in an unbelievable way—it was instantly clear that we'd struck gold.

By the end of 2020, like so many others, I'd put on a lot of pandemic weight *and* let myself slip back into drinking. After getting into the rhythm of two or three drinks every night—on top of going out to party with David—on January first I at least decided to quit drinking for the month. I'd partied very hard on our quarantined New Year's Eve at home—we'd hung little disco lights, played music, and cooked an unbelievable steak-and-seafood spread. Even Beckham had had a great time dancing to the music, watching his mom drink way too much. When I woke up hungover on the first day of 2021, I also resolved to clean up my eating.

Soon I'd lost a substantial amount of weight, and fasting was helping with my digestive issues—my SIBO had kicked back in, and I was again taking Xifaxan to kill off the bacteria that was once again attempting to conquer my intestine. Most days I wasn't eating until about one or two o'clock in the afternoon. Before too long, I'd gotten back down to a size zero and 120 pounds, which I loved. I looked the best I had in a long time, but I have to admit that a lot of it was stress driven. The pounds kept falling off to the point where it became unhealthy—I even started losing my hair and breaking out.

By our next quarterly event in July, I was still sober, but it'd otherwise been a very, very stressful quarter. We'd grown to twenty-five employees, were making $300,000 consistently month over month, and were quickly approaching the $400,000 threshold. I decided to take an Uber and have a margarita on our first night out as a team—my first drink of the entire new year. Our team had an amazing Mexican dinner, then went to a Russian vodka place for another handful of drinks.

I knew when it was time to leave, and when I left, I encouraged everyone else to call it a night too. For obvious reasons, I have a very strict policy on drinking and driving with the employees—everyone's allowed to put rideshares on their corporate cards, and we also offer to pay for everyone's overnight garage parking if need be. After drinking responsibly that night, I went home and I started to tell myself, *Maybe I'm okay being a CEO of a nearly $4 million company with twenty-five employees. Maybe I* can *make this part of my identity.*

So, again, against my better judgment, I resumed drinking while going all in at work. I absolutely threw myself behind investing in our growth. By that time I was working with a full executive team: COO, CRO, CMO, CSO. The five of us were unified in the mission of taking the company to $5 million, then $10 million, then $20 million.

I'd joined a different CEO group in 2021 and come back from our discussions with a vision to grow the company to $13 million in thirteen years. Even that felt conservative—I knew we could do it a lot faster than that. I remember how happy, grateful, and even relieved Henry was when I came back to tell him I was on that path—I'd finally admitted aloud that I was willing to exit the company.

His response was measured. "Okay. Thirteen years is a long time. That'll take me into my late thirties—I can handle that. I'll stick around. Without an end date, I didn't know how long I could be a part of this. I really needed to know that we were working toward something specific." When I saw how happy he was, I instantly realized how important *his* happiness was to my own. In no time, we were exploring scenarios for an exit after seven or even five years.

As our growth goals got more aggressive, we put together new lines of businesses and formed a huge new top-line revenue goal—all against my better judgment. Guess what I started to do next? I started to *worship* that top-line revenue goal. Yet again, the business became my idol. I started to think about all the millions of dollars I was going to have—I was already spending it in my mind. The worship of money crept back in, and with it, the greed, the envy, and all the other sinful things I'd managed to discard flooded back into my life. I was still drinking when we approached the $5 million mark as a company two months in advance of our four-year anniversary. *Wow, Mary. Pat on the back. Aren't you special?*

Next, we won the prestigious Colorado Companies to Watch award. Thousands of companies apply each year, and only fifty win. Moreover, once you win, you're "a winner" forever, a permanent inductee into the local business community. When we found out we won, we had to keep it secret because they announce it at a big gala. *Wow, Mary. What an accomplishment.*

Though we should have been basking in all the recognition, I was approaching complete burnout. At the same time, we started getting negative feedback from our clients for the very first time. Mostly, the complaints related to our new junior-level employees, many of whom didn't yet know how to do some of the most basic tasks of marketing. As our executive leaders were forced to redo their subordinates' work, the mess got bigger and bigger, which caused everyone's quality of life to sink. Reality started to sink in: *We're in over our heads.*

> **Though we should have been basking in all the recognition, I was approaching complete burnout.**

Of course, not everything we did was bad. We had plenty of great successes in 2021. We'd scaled to working with eleven companies that year, up from nine in 2020. We had incredible ROI and success stories—in fact, better than ever. But at the same time, some of the people we were working with—start-ups, and our new marketing-only engagements—we had no business working with. Those clients weren't happy, and as a result, I was starting to have to give out refunds. Every time I did, that old thought came back: *What happened to my business? This isn't the company I built.*

The stress became so intense that I had to ask Paul to cover my back. He'd bravely moved his family to Denver from Los Angeles, and after he'd uprooted himself, I'd never truly set him up for success. Though we had an org chart and a plan, I was thoroughly burned out.

I called Paul in to save me from drowning without truly prepping, training, managing, or mentoring him, and in so doing, I set him up for failure. I just threw him into the role, assuming he'd figure it out. The plan was to basically split my job in two. I wanted to focus on leadership and business development while leaving Paul to manage our client engagements and the VPs, while Henry comanaged the junior marketers.

As Paul took on the CRO role in October, I started to realize how mentally unwell I was. A lot of my focus shifted to trying to set him up for success, while figuring out what exactly my job was now that he'd stepped in to take over so much of my work. Once again, I'd been neglecting my family to focus on my business and was mad at myself for it.

In August, I made a commitment: *Come hell or high water, I'm taking my son to school every day, then I'm picking him up.* I refused to turn into the person I had been, but all along I was lying to myself—I already *was* back to who I had been. My son needed to be dropped off at eight and picked up at three. In theory, I was trying to work from eight thirty to two fifteen, but in practice, that was a joke. The business needed me from six in the morning to eight o'clock at night, easily eighty to ninety hours a week.

So as the school year began, I started cutting out of work at two fifteen to pick up Beckham, but that didn't stop everybody from needing me around the clock for a hundred different things. After I'd picked up my son, he'd just sit there watching TV while I completely ignored him in favor of taking calls, working on my laptop, and writing emails. Worse, I could see it breaking his heart. Over and over, he'd ask, *Mommy, when are you going to be done working?*

Starting kindergarten was a pivotal point in my son's life, and I wanted to be the mom who picked him up, spent afternoons with him, played with him, took him to the park, and talked with him about his day. Instead, I threw him in front of the TV and hid out in my office. Of course, he didn't know how to cope. He didn't know how to work the TV remote and would just sit there crying out of helplessness. Mommy would be on a call, and he didn't know how to skip through a commercial or change to a different video. I'd walk out of the office between calls to see my son sitting there with red puppy eyes, crying because his mom was completely neglecting him.

By that point, I was broken. My internal monologue had become *I'm not doing anything well, and now I'm falling apart at the seams.* Even David was working a ton of overtime, including every other Saturday, so he wasn't home much either. I'd try to manage until six or seven at night, at which point I'd be utterly exhausted, on the verge of a mental breakdown. Asking Paul to step into the CRO role wasn't as much of a promotion for him as it was a break for me. I desperately needed his help.

After Paul had been in his new role for three weeks, I stepped away and took a family trip to Disneyland during Beckham's fall break, and there I finally fell apart. From the second we got in the car, I knew it'd be a disaster. I was already distraught, short tempered, and frustrated. My depression and anxiety were off the charts. The demons had not only fully crept back in but were completely in control.

On the road to the airport, I immediately got in a fight with my son—my *five-year-old son.* I was driving, and he said something that set me off, and I snapped back at him. What mother snaps at their son en route to the airport on a trip to *Disneyland*, of all places? Even worse, I couldn't stop myself—I just kept unloading about how mad I was at my husband *and* my son, how unappreciated I felt, how I was being taken advantage of.

Of course, none of that was true. If anything, my husband and son were the ones supporting *me.* When we got onto the airplane, I just put headphones on and hid under my mask and my hat, listened to depressing music, and cried for the entire flight. After we checked into the resort, we went straight to the pool, where I ordered the first of many drinks. Though I hadn't eaten all day, I just started slamming one after another.

Before long, I was drunkenly unloading on David again, in front of everyone. I started yelling about how I had no support, how I hated *his* job and the fact that he was even still working. At the time, we were making plenty of money from my business alone.

"You don't even *have* to work. I don't understand why you don't quit, if only to help me out with drop-offs and pickups. I'm *trying*, but I can't do it all. My company's out of control, and you're doing nothing to help me." The more I laid into him, the more people around the pool started staring at us. I went on and on about how Beckham wouldn't let me work. "He's always so distraught. He shuts my laptop and begs me not to make phone calls."

This is all heartbreaking to even recall—what kind of mom was I? My son was crying for help and needed a mother, and I was blaming *him*. Nevertheless, I stormed back up to the hotel room, drunk on an empty stomach, careening into another breakdown. I went to bed and left my husband and son on their own for the night.

The next morning I woke numb inside and out, mortified that I'd spoken to my husband that way. Still, I hid behind my mask and my sunglasses and my hat and spent the day sullenly standing in line at all the rides without saying a word to anyone. The whole time, David kept trying to check on me. Thankfully, toward the end of that day, I started to come out of the funk a little bit and had mostly calmed down by nighttime.

Then, against my better judgment, we went back to the pool, where I ordered a couple more drinks. Somehow, I managed to keep my cool. David and I started to talk, and I apologized for my behavior. I broke down and told him how much I hated my company, my job, and everything I'd built.

He could've told me he was right all along, but of course, and as always, he was so kind. "You just put Paul in your role. Can't you just walk away? Take a step back and let the executive team run the show. Take some time off to take care of yourself."

Though I wasn't ready and didn't know how to do it, we tried to make a plan. GG offered to help pick up Beckham one day a week, and we also decided to enroll Beckham in an after-school program. That filled me with guilt—all his *friends'* moms managed to pick their kids up at three, but I just had to come around to the fact that asking for help was okay.

Gradually, I was able to back away from work. Paul stepped fully into my position, and my five senior executives worked their magic. All that was left for me was business development. Believe it

No business should cause that much stress and strain, especially beyond the start-up phase.

or not, things actually started running more smoothly—or at least what *felt* like smoothly. In reality, Paul simply became my filter for all the chaos, struggle, and strife within the company. Instead of me absorbing it directly, it all just redirected straight to Paul.

Naturally, *his* quality of life consequently started deteriorating, and all the while I had no idea—he was so proud to be in his role and was such a brilliant leader, and everyone loved him, but he started to bear the brunt of our failure to build a solid business. No business should cause that much stress and strain, especially beyond the start-up phase. We should have been plateauing a bit, allowing ourselves a couple of good, smooth years before figuring out whether we wanted to actually grow more.

Meanwhile, Henry was still rabidly trying to build infrastructure, and two other executives were pouring their hearts into the company wherever needed. I'd stepped away to the extent that I was only involved in doing inbound business development, and that only took six to eight hours a week. I was still dabbling in accounting and payroll, as well as doing speaking engagements and podcasts, which I love, but gradually, I not only started to feel bored but that my value within my own organization had fizzled out.

I started looking into investing in another company—the opportunity fell into my lap. It was a great consumer packaged goods (CPG) brand that I'd discovered through one of our clients. They sold clothing and accessories, which was novel and interesting, and were already on their way to scaling toward a $10 million exit. I'd made so much money that year that I became increasingly interested in investing to the point of 51 percent ownership.

That all seemed like a lot of fun, mostly because I was looking to fill the void left by vacating my role in my own company—the value of *me* in my own company was gone. I was no longer our face internally, nor was I managing any employees. I'd been reduced to stocking the refrigerator with drinks and filling the snack bin, making sure the office was tidy. After going full tilt for so long and then transitioning into work that was so meaningless, I started to hate it.

A whole new level of depression set in. I felt like I was losing my identity. On one hand, this new season was a breath of fresh air, because the stress I'd been dealing with was gone. I was spending far more time at home and had instantaneously become a better mom and wife all over again. But all my stress was replaced by a deeper longing to be somewhere where I was valued. When the CPG company saw value in me, I simply couldn't resist.

Then, without warning, one of my employees filed a sexual harassment complaint against two people on our leadership team. I was dumbfounded and stunned that something like that would happen inside of my organization and initially thought it had to be a false claim. Then, when I looked deeper, I found out that it was true.

I was appalled, and the whole episode rocked my world. I couldn't believe that something like this had happened at the hands of people whom I'd trusted with my company and my brand. They knew who I was and what I'm about—I'm an outspokenly faith-based leader and a conservative Christian woman and always made a point of leading with empathy, love, and grace. What transpired was deeply inappropriate, and though it happened off the clock and at a private event that had nothing to do with work, everyone involved worked for me, and therefore it was a liability I couldn't escape.

My attorney was working around the clock, figuring out what to do. I was immediately advised to move forward with separation, which broke my heart. I also had to pay a large settlement, which hurt our bottom line. I'd loved those two departing leaders and couldn't imagine the company without them. The whole ordeal was so hard to stomach or even understand, both for me and the entire team. The whole thing heightened the disconnect I'd already been feeling—I couldn't stop thinking, *This isn't the company I created. I'm better than this. My* company *is better than this.* All the while, I also couldn't help but get more and more down on *myself.*

In the end, I gave my remaining executives, including Henry, the reins to run the company, and David and I ultimately passed on becoming investors in the CPG company. I knew I needed to find a position that put me in a seat of value again, or my days at my own company were numbered. Something had to give.

CHAPTER

21

CHAPTER 21

After our ill-fated trip to Disneyland, I knew deep down that I needed to quit drinking for good but didn't take steps to do so immediately. When we came back, we had a quarterly event with the team after becoming one of Colorado's companies to watch. I'd pulled myself together enough to realize that I hadn't been well or a great person to be around in general, so I really wanted to make that awards ceremony a special night for my team.

We all went downtown for a preevent, ordered a bottle of champagne and some cocktails, and started drinking, taking photos, and having a great time. We walked to the event, and our formal wear drew all kinds of attention downtown; then we entered the event on a red carpet. I'd ordered a stunning ombre purple-and-pink ball gown that I was so excited to wear, and after we took pictures, we were shown to our table, where everyone started drinking wine.

When we accepted the award onstage, our team was cheering so loud. Afterward, back at our table, a prospective client came up to say hello, congratulate us, introduce us to some of his leadership team, and have a brief business conversation. At that point I'd been partying for three hours, was starting to slur my words, and couldn't come off the high enough to have a serious conversation. Then it dawned on me: I was in a room *entirely full of prospective clients*, yet I was solely focused on celebrating and having a great time. That was it for me. *This* was the night I would stop drinking.

But after the gala, we went to a rooftop bar and celebrated with yet another round of drinks. Finally, David turned to me and suggested we call it a night, and I'm so grateful that he did. As the CEO of the company, I needed to set an example, if only for our younger staff. I wanted people to see that it's okay to go home. *You don't have to party into the wee hours.* I was bummed in that wonderful moment to leave, but I'm grateful to this day that we did.

When I woke up in the morning, I knew I was done. That was my last night drinking. If I was going to be serious about my mental health journey, getting out of my depressive state, and curing my anxiety, I had to be very serious about decluttering my life and my health.

That was the last night that I've had anything to drink. I don't know if I'll ever drink again, but I don't have any plans to. At this point, I don't need anything to alter my state. I'd rather get my life in check to the extent that I don't feel the *need* to drink or use any form of drug. A relaxing bubble bath is nice from time to time, but that's just about all I need at this point.

I had a sober Thanksgiving, a sober Christmas, and a sober New Year's. I was still doing business development for House of Revenue when a SaaS start-up called Spotz came into our pipeline—they were like an Airbnb for community spaces: churches, restaurants, community centers, fields, parks, libraries, museums, extra office space, meeting rooms, and more.

By that point, we'd collectively vowed to never work with start-ups again—they're so volatile by nature, and we'd been burned by one after another. But there was something different about this one, its founder, their team, their technology, and their vision. Something made me want to take a crack at it. No one on my own team shared my excitement, so I told them, *Okay, fine. Then I'll handle it.* I became their fractional CRO and fell in love with their team, and within a couple of months I wanted to become a full-on investor in the company.

I was sitting on some extra cash after closing the year out strong—David and I had made more money than we'd ever made that year, on top of selling that farmhouse. I wrote a check for $55,000 to invest in my first company and was over the moon to be a sitting investor *and* their fractional CRO.

Then, another interesting client came into our queue—a services business, similar to our own. Paul and I agreed to kick off that project together, and together we flew to Michigan, where I fell in love all over again. They were faith-based, outspoken Christians, prayed before their team meetings, and everything was scripture based—all of which I loved. I liked how they thought, how they managed, and how they worked together. Their mission felt close to my heart, and I thought I could add a lot of value to their enterprise, so I became *their* stand-in VP until we found someone perfect to replace me.

Before long, their cofounders had a disagreement and couldn't see eye to eye, and it knocked the entire engagement sideways. I didn't know exactly how to navigate the situation but still wanted to see it through. In hindsight, I should have just stepped away.

At that point, I had two of my own clients, and Paul was mostly acting as our CEO. He was still technically the CRO but was running the all-hands meetings and had become the face of the company. Meanwhile, Henry was doing a phenomenal job running operations. The two of them were a great team, and business was humming along. By the time spring break rolled around, I had some time for reflection. David, Beckham, and I drove from Denver to Waco, got a little

Airbnb downtown in a renovated farmhouse, and had an absolute dream of a week. I unplugged, truly took time off, from both of my clients, and enjoyed the quality time with my family.

In the background, I was increasingly aware of how challenging it had become for me to work within the systems and processes introduced to the company in my absence. We'd created a lot of red tape for ourselves, and it made it hard to do our jobs. I was also struggling to work with our new people. We'd shifted under Henry's plan to hiring more junior-level team members, all of whom were far earlier in their careers. Up until that point, I'd always expected to have things done and done right. Now there was a lot of management, explanation, training, development, and general handholding even to get simple tasks done, and it was eating up my time.

I came back from vacation like a bull in a china shop.

With all this in mind, I came back from vacation like a bull in a china shop. I entered hot into a meeting with Paul and Henry and was accusatory, demanding, judgmental, and stern about what had been built in my absence. That caused an argument, and it's one of my greatest regrets in our relationship to this day. I take full ownership for not handling that situation better, and to be clear, I still have nothing but love and appreciation for those two. I'll always see them as two of the most talented revenue leaders and business professionals I've ever worked with.

At that point, we'd *all* been working with Doug, the business coach, together. I called him after our argument and told him, "I'm done. I'm done with the business. I can't do this anymore."

"Why?"

"I have to trust my intuition. I'm trying to listen to my gut. I'm a very dynamic person. I'm passionate, outspoken, high pace, high urgency, high capacity. I burn a lot of people out. It's not just workloads or speed—I think people get tired of me. I'm a lot to handle, especially in a work environment. I can be a lot to handle personally too. I'm grateful for my husband and my marriage, because he's really grown to understand me and we make a beautiful pair. I've learned to submit to him as I do to the Lord, and now we have a beautiful marriage.

"But at work, I'm the boss. I'm in charge. At the end of the day, the money comes from me. Payroll comes from me—our paychecks are cut from money in *my* account. There isn't a lot of room for mistakes. You can only finance mistakes for so long, and if the runway ends, you go into debt or have to bring on a partner. And I definitely don't want to do either of those things." I went on to highlight everything that I thought was wrong with our model and the company in general. I came back from six months on the sidelines wanting to make changes, and they wanted to stay the course.

"It takes time," they told me.

"We don't *have* time."

More and more, clients were starting to try to cancel our services. Two tried to back out after only a few months and were busy lawyering up. Three or four others were up for renewal and opted out, and in the past, 90 percent or more of our clients had renewed. Without more renewals, we had a sudden, urgent need for business development, which fell on me, but I already had my hands full with my two full-time clients. Meanwhile, we were burning money on our new VP, who was sitting there without clients to work with.

All of a sudden, we were in a bad way, and I saw the writing on the wall. I knew I had to put my head down and focus on business development. I wanted to transition back to our old model and axe all the junior people—it'd initially be more expensive, but it'd also allow us to charge more for better results. But Henry and Paul had worked so hard building out their new model, and they wouldn't budge. Even Doug thought I was being drastic.

In that meeting, Henry and Paul looked at and spoke to me in a way that they never had before. Up to that point, they'd always looked up to me, and always with love in their eyes. We'd always had a very caring relationship, and now that we weren't seeing eye to eye, it made me feel like they'd simply had enough of me. As always, I couldn't stand to be where I wasn't valued or appreciated. God created me with unique gifts and talents, and I cannot accept being dormant. I have to keep moving.

I couldn't stand to be where I wasn't valued or appreciated.

I want to do great things in this world, and I want to spread the good news of the gospel to the ends of the earth. Of all places, God has chosen to put me in the marketplace. I want that to be somewhere where I get to serve him, honor him, spread the good news of his name, be his light to the people around me, and show people what his love, grace, mercy, and kindness look like.

I can't do any of that successfully while hating my job, dreading going in to work, or being utterly opposed to the people on my team. So I called my business broker and told him, *Let's list the business.* When I came home to tell David, he was shocked.

"There has to be another way. You love this company, and you love Paul and Henry."

"I do, but we're not seeing eye to eye anymore. I love that they're so fully in their roles. I just need to get out of the way and let them do this. I don't want to be around if they're going to grow this into something that looks like an agency."

He was still dumbfounded after we talked it out, but I met with my broker and settled on a $4 million asking price. When we put the business on the market, it got a lot of attention. We had several inquiries, had half a dozen meetings, and ended up with two letters of interest, one higher than the other. Naturally, I took the higher of the two.

At that point, my heart was so conflicted, because I felt like Paul and Henry should have a say in who the new owner would be. I still wanted to do whatever I possibly could to make them happy and to ensure they had everything they needed to fulfill their wildest dreams. I just wanted to take care of them and wanted them to be grateful that I was in their life, instead of disappointed. Again, it came out of that need to be loved that I've carried my whole life, all of which grew out of not feeling loved as a child.

Paul and Henry had respect for me, and I wanted them to love me, and I thought that I could *earn* that by making sure that they were involved in the sales process and picking the new owner. I could have washed my hands of the thing, cut and run. In every book I've ever read about selling a business, rule number one is *Do not tell any of your employees.* But when I talked to Doug again, I told him, "I have to tell them. I just cannot do this without them knowing."

There I was, in my own conflict with my own executive team, still working with my client in Michigan whose founders were in conflict, still trying to help scale Spotz. In the meantime, I'd invested in yet *another* company. I'd met the founder of a plastic-free vegan supplement company, and decided to become an angel investor at $25,000, simply trying to create a bright spot anywhere I could. When things are going rough, I can't help but add fuel to the fire to make things even more complicated.

As I had a buyer on the line at $4 million for my own company, I realized that I'd soon be out of work. In April, I reached out to Sabrina, who had been a tremendous asset to the company all along. We went to dinner, and I told her everything: all about the tension between me, Paul, and Henry; selling the company; and wanting to just get out of the way. I told her I wanted to go into business with her, where we could be fractional CRO and CMO in a new partnership. I wanted to move my contract with Spotz to the new business, continue scaling companies, put in our own investments, and split the returns. Sabrina looked at me and said, "Wherever you go, I go."

I felt so much comfort in that moment. I felt like I had a *plan*. In hindsight, that's a weakness of mine. I'm fearless, but I don't thrive in the world of gray. I don't like ambiguity. I need black and white. I could never go a day without having the next thing in place. In hindsight, I wish that I'd just slowed down and let the Lord work. Instead, I had to pretend that I was the one with the answer to everything. I can't ever be patient. I can't rely on God or have the patience to wait for him to work in my life. It's one of my worst tendencies and perhaps the main one where I struggle to show obedience to him.

There's so much scripture about waiting on the Lord, submitting our plans to him, allowing *his* will to be done, yet I had to stop everything and create an entirely new business just to make sure I was protected and taking care of myself. It's a shame. Had I waited on the Lord, his plans would've been revealed and his will would have been done. His will for my life is good and pleasing. When I don't wait, or fail to lean into my trust for him, I confuse what I think he wants for me with what I'm able to do myself, and from there come all kinds of problems.

In any case, Sabrina and I came up with a name for our company, and we bought the URLs right then and there. I knew we were going to talk business, so I'd brought my laptop—I was that person in the nice restaurant with my laptop open, buying domains, emailing attorneys, filing for a trademark, and transferring money over for the retainer to build out an operating agreement, all right there at the dinner table.

When I woke up the next day, I felt so much peace. When I talked to Doug, I told him, "I have to tell Paul and Henry. Everyone's advised me not to do it, but I don't think it's possible. I care about them too much. They need to know." I felt all this from the pit of my stomach. I can't lie, even if I try—I have the worst poker face ever. They'd know something was up, and I didn't want them to be blindsided and find out from anyone other than me.

In the end, Doug encouraged me. "If that's what you feel, trust your intuition."

Then, unfortunately, the tension that had been building all along boiled into another argument in our next executive meeting. The argument started when I asked Paul to follow up on the status of one of our invoices that hadn't been paid on time. That had pushed our receivable into the next month and hurt our projections. I had been very focused on tightening up on expenses—we needed to be super frugal until we got our ducks in a row. Paul and Henry didn't understand why I was suddenly becoming so conscious about our financials.

After trying to be so thoughtful, I ended up snapping. I lost it and stormed out of the meeting, and I'm not usually one to do that. I just want to be a happy, loving, kind person, but my fuse was so short. Everything was triggering me, and every day felt like an uphill battle. I felt like I was living a double life, carrying around this big secret, fearful that I wouldn't be able to manipulate the situation so that everyone could walk away happy, scared of being devastated if I let anyone down.

When our quarterly meeting came around, I mostly just sat back. I did a little state of the union, told people that I was enjoying becoming an investor, that I'd started a little side company with Sabrina to explore investing in companies and scaling them for bigger exits. When it became clear that I planned on stepping away even further, it made a few team members distraught—I found out later that they'd come to work for us in the first place because of me.

When my original buyer saw that our numbers weren't trending up, it made him cautious. He lowered his offer to $1.9 million, to which I said, "No, thank you"—our backup offer exceeded $3 million. But there was a problem. The first buyer wanted to be a distant owner and more of a capital investor, uninvolved with running the company. That was good for Paul and Henry, because they'd remain CEO and COO, which was beautiful for their careers.

The backup buyer wanted to work *inside* of the company as CEO and CMO, which created overlap with Paul and Henry. Paul was a phenomenal CRO, but he'd really been eyeing the CEO position, and it would've been a great fit for him. The new buyer might have killed that upward trajectory for Paul, *and* put Henry's position in jeopardy.

The Thursday before Memorial Day weekend, I had another meeting with the backup buyer. I gushed about the company, where we were headed, and how great an opportunity this was going to be. They asked me to stick around for a little bit to manage the transition, which I was happy to do.

From there, I went in to meet with Henry. Both of our emotions were on high, and it was a tough conversation. He thought I was a fool for selling the company. He thought that if I could just stick it out for one to two more years, we'd grow substantially and be able to exit at $5 million to $10 million, if not more. He couldn't wrap his head around why I would walk away for so little for something he thought was worth so much more.

I looked at him in all sincerity and said, "Because I hate my job, and I hate my life. This is the unhappiest I've been in a long time. I don't *want* to work here. I don't want to be associated with this, and no amount of money can fix that. I'll take whatever I can get for the business so I can move on and start over, because I don't want any part of this."

It wasn't intentional, but of course it hurt his feelings to hear that. He'd worked tirelessly to build the company up and had such a vision. The guy had absolutely poured his heart and his soul into the company and done everything that he possibly could for it to be successful. When those words came out of my mouth, I think I probably shattered our relationship, because I think all along that he felt like he was doing it for *me*, not for him, so *I* could have a big, successful exit. It was one of the worst conversations we'd ever had, and it certainly didn't end well.

Later that day, I went to my next meeting with Paul. I was so excited to tell him about how much I'd built him up with the new buyer and how excited they were to work with him. Then, when I did, he was obviously unsettled and unhappy. I tried to talk him into taking a position as president, but he was naturally disappointed, and the damage was done. Everything I'd feared had come true.

Then, some light pierced the clouds. Paul proposed that he and Henry could buy the company. Instantly, my exact words were, "There's no one else I'd rather sell it to." I introduced them to my broker. Paul said he'd try to pull everything together over the coming Memorial Day weekend. When Tuesday came, instead of waking up to their intent to purchase, I received both Paul's and Henry's resignations, one right after the other. They both gave a lot of notice so as not to leave me high and dry—they were going to spend the summer with the company to ensure we could make the transition.

I drove into the office numb, and when I arrived, I went immediately into fight or flight. First, I made a point of sitting with every team member and told them how excited I was to be pivoting and reinvolving myself with the company, getting reacclimated with the team, and stepping back in as CEO. Naturally, everyone was pretty surprised, but there was also a good deal of relief, because some of the team had been expecting me to step down that week.

Paul had a new client kickoff scheduled for that day, and I would've loved for him to help because I wasn't at all prepared for it. Everything was just so fresh and difficult, so I told him to take the day off. It was a very scary time. I added an all-hands meeting to our calendar and started to think about how I was going to tell my team what had happened. On top of that, I had a bunch of large expenses coming up and no idea how I'd pay for them. Outside of work, I was launching two podcasts, and my personal branding agency was publishing in full force. I knew I couldn't keep up that expense, so I terminated our contract.

I thought I had a plan—those famous last words.

I thought I had a plan—those famous last words. God has a better plan. Only God knows what's best for us. No matter how hard I try to make things happen, there's only one who makes all things happen. Despite everything, sometimes I'm still foolish enough to believe that *I'm* in control and that it's my bare hands and brilliant mind that makes things happen. My selfish world had been turned upside down, and I had no idea how to start doing damage control. My relationships with my clients and team members were on the rocks, *and* my plate was still full.

That June turned into a hellish, nightmarish month. Again, I found myself working seven-day, hundred-hour weeks to save the business. Still, I tried to paint a vision for the future. Sabrina became my right hand, and we started making changes right away. Most of that came back to ripping out the superfluous infrastructure that'd been making it so unnecessarily hard to do our jobs. It was all too complex, too detailed, too rigid. We'd lost room for creativity. When I point-blank asked each and every employee what changes they wanted to see, the number one answer was to pare all those processes down, so that was the first thing we did.

At a broader level, we envisioned a path to start playing for upside commission payouts with our clients, instead of just retainer fees, and planned further to eventually play for equity and even larger payouts. To do either, we needed to build up our cash reserves and store up our acorns. So we built a new model, reduced staff, and reduced the client count for each team from three to two so they could put in more quality time with each. From there, we focused on righting our relationships, both with our clients and within our team. We couldn't salvage all our clients, so we offered refunds and early contract exits. Then we gave overworked team members the big vacations they so badly needed.

When I talked to Spotz, they understood that I needed to divert my attention back toward my own business for at least the next sixty days. When I talked to the other company in Michigan, we agreed that it would be better to dissolve our contract and walk away.

We tried to take a family vacation that June to David and Beckham's N scale train convention in Nashville, but for me it wasn't much of a vacation. I was simply not able to unplug. I brought my laptop to a lot of the events and whipped it out in the car to work while we were driving, and it even came with me to auction night.

Then, finally, over the Fourth of July weekend, after five straight hundred-hour weeks, I finally unplugged. Once again, I'd completely neglected my family, and once again, I was upset with myself about it.

When the weekend was through, I threw myself right back in the trenches. By the end of July, my personal expenses were mounting from every angle. I'd had a grand plan in mind for everything, except for where the money would come from. Meanwhile, employees were starting to resign. We lost a few key team members, and our pipeline was slowing.

Russia invaded Ukraine, and like so many companies, we hit a perfect storm. Inflation shot up, interest rates rose, the market slowed down, and the economy became a big question mark. Everyone, from me to my employees, started freaking out about inflation.

Because our junior staff members had called the company's competence into question, I knew we had to bring in the best of the best to set things straight. I was spending a lot of money on our high-level roles, and good people are expensive. David and I were having to pull from savings to cover basic living expenses. All the while, both our clients and our employees were demanding more.

Our margins were pinched, and the company was upside down. Lost revenue ate through our cash reserves. Toward the end of July and early August, it looked like everything was going to come crashing down, and I was really feeling the weight and pressure. I tried to focus on bringing new clients on board, and we ultimately gained two in August, which allowed us to implement pay increases for everyone. A nice wave of leads came in thereafter, but I failed to close on any of them. I was shocked—we'd always had a solid 50 percent closing rate.

I went to speak at Inbound, HubSpot's big annual conference in Boston. I'd always managed to pull in leads there, but this time around, I only came home with one, and nothing came of it. Everyone was tightening their purses—you could just feel it. I remember being with Sabrina in our hotel room in a total state of panic.

Meanwhile, one of our new clients—again, a start-up—was dealing with the same issues within the market. They'd lost their top investor and hundreds of thousands of dollars, and they simply couldn't afford to pay us. When they ran out of money, it just put me over the edge. We'd worked so hard to bring them on and had just lost our last five deals.

I came back from the conference knowing I'd have to have a really difficult conversation with my team about resorting to plan B, which meant processing three layoffs, each very difficult, and making room for three new C-level executives. We simply needed all the expertise we could get.

So 2022 wasn't even over, and it had already been one of the most hellacious years of my life. I didn't enjoy coming to work one single day. Each was an uphill battle. It comes back to not liking or wanting the CEO title. I've told my CROs multiple times: *I just want to be your peer.* I don't want to be a CEO. I flat-out don't want the power or the responsibility. I don't want people to fear me because I hold their jobs, pay, and livelihoods in my hands. I hate all that. In the end, I just want to have fun at work.

In our plan B meeting, I realized that I was trying to have a C-level conversation, trying to be transparent about our financial situation and the plan. But when I looked around, all I saw was fear in my people's eyes. It then hit me on another level how lonely it can be to be a CEO. When times are lean, the executives surrounding you probably aren't going to say, *Yeah, we get it. How can we support you? What do you need?* Instead, they're thinking about how they're going to protect their families and whether they're going to lose their jobs.

As a CEO, when work is fun, there's so much camaraderie. You're building relationships with your peers, and on the good days, you feel like everyone is all in. People have extreme ownership, and they're thinking like owners, not employees. Then, when the going gets tough, adversity reveals how people truly feel and where their loyalty is.

As a CEO, when work is fun, there's so much camaraderie. Then, when the going gets tough, adversity reveals how people truly feel and where their loyalty is.

I'm not saying any of this is necessarily a bad thing—I've had to consider how I'd feel in *their* shoes. Would I have the loyalty to go up to *my* CEO and ask, *How can I help you? What do you need? How do we solve this problem? What can I do?* Or, as breadwinner, would my instinct be for self-preservation? Would I go straight back to my family? To myself?

As a CEO, you expect to be surrounded by people of immense professional maturity, but you have to remember: all the people around you are still your employees. As much as I want my people to act with an ownership mentality and to stand by my side, it's a fundamentally unrealistic expectation. These people have spouses and children, and they need to put their families first. Looking around, I couldn't help but think, *I guess I can't have it all.*

CHAPTER 22

CHAPTER 22

I should've kept my company small. I should have trusted my instinct. I should have stayed strong in my spiritual walk. I should not have scaled it or adopted someone else's vision. The Lord and I had rebuilt the company in 2020, and then I took what we rebuilt and turned it on its head, and I started obsessing over money, growth, scaling, recognition, and that potential multimillion-dollar exit. All the things the Lord *didn't* want me focusing on collectively became my north star, stole my joy, and led to nothing but fear, anxiety, depression, and suffering.

We put forth a lot of effort over the summer to turn things around, and while the summer was rough, September was worse. After drawing a line in the sand between junior and senior employees, those layoffs further rocked the boat, as I knew they would. As soon as word got out, two more employees I didn't anticipate losing resigned. One was among our most tenured employees, and the other was a young marketer, a bright, shining star. They both gave four weeks' notice, and by the end of those four weeks I felt like I'd been hit by a two-by-four.

Then, another client had skipped out on a $20,000 final bill, and I had to take them to court in what became my very first lawsuit. We'd done beautiful work for them, and they were claiming, with no basis, that one of my former employees had waived their fee. That same employee is still a friend of mine, and they shot that claim right down.

Meanwhile, another client chose to terminate *their* contract early while also relentlessly sending me harassing emails—each below the belt, rude, nasty, and mean, accusing me of being a fake Christian who used Jesus to close a sale. I ended up having to turn *that* over to my attorney as well, who threatened to file a restraining order.

To throw fuel on the fire, another team member recommended we off-board another client because they'd gone off in a different direction and didn't quite fit the bill for what our company was meant to do. When we let them out of their contract, another $20,000 per month went out the window. The layoffs and resignations had at least freed up a little cash to stay in business, but we were losing so much money that I wasn't sure if we'd be able to keep the lights on.

When October rolled around, I felt a strange sense of relief: *Okay. New month. I can do this. I can do this.* I doubled down and threw myself into business development, bringing on new team members and clients. As I'd been feeling so down and defeated, I'd reached out to another female CEO with her own private equity firm to ask for some CEO real talk. I simply didn't know what to do, so I went for a walk, called her, and poured my heart out to her.

"I feel like I'm doing it all wrong. The mixture of the economy, inflation, clients demanding more, employees demanding more, lack of margin, losing money, people sending me hateful emails—I don't think I can do this anymore."

She gave me a desperately needed pep talk, reaffirmed her belief in our company and how much she loved working with us, and reminded me of the tremendous work we'd done for *her* clients. She wanted to send us three $250,000 deals before the end of the year and said that if we gave her a discount, she'd prepay for them. That meant a nice discount for her and a much-needed cash injection into our bank account—enough to effectively solve our immediate short-term problems.

The prospect of that deal just about lifted everything off me, pulled me out of my funk, gave me hope, *and* made me realize that all I was *really* facing was a cash problem. In other words, I simply needed to *sell* my way out of this. Unfortunately, that deal with her never even came into fruition, but not for lack of trying—she had her own challenges, dealing with her own distressed clients, and a lot more. What mattered more was the injection of hope and new energy.

Around the same time, a phenomenal former client named Payroll Network reached back out to us. Their VP of sales, whom we'd worked with in 2020, had resigned, so I decided to throw myself into helping them for ten or fifteen hours a week. That got a flow of cash coming in, and I loved working with them—it was a huge breath of fresh air after all the hateful emails I'd been receiving. They're so kind and professional *and* really valued and appreciated me. They invited me out to their office in Maryland to get the lay of the land, and I had a great time. I was so in my element—after all, they're a payroll company, and I know the business inside and out.

Then, we got yet another client cancellation from yet another client—they'd grown their revenue after we did great work for them, and they wanted out with two months left on their contract. They claimed we didn't do what we set out to do, which was utter blasphemy. It felt like the economy had become so tight that people were looking for any means possible to wiggle out of their contracts.

This all led to a very difficult meeting. There was no terminable cause in our contract, yet they were telling me they were no longer doing business with us. I had to tell them, "That's not an option, because there's no termination clause." This led to a very heated argument over email. They were quite adamant that they weren't working with us anymore, and my position was, *Why have a contract in the first place if you're just going to ignore it?* When I ultimately just let them out of their contract, I had to speak to the team member in charge of their engagement. She'd worked so hard to help them grow revenue and to lead their team and was absolutely devastated and in tears that they would do this to her, or us.

Then, yet another of our clients wanted out of their contract. They, too, claimed we hadn't done the work we were hired to do, all after we'd exceeded their already ambitious Q3 goals by 30 percent. They called me into their office to meet with them on October 31, and I had to stand up for myself and say, "That's simply not true."

I was accused of raising my voice in a threatening tone and was kicked out of their office. I couldn't believe it. I got in my car and cried hysterically the entire way home, gutted from the inside out. I was coming off of months of hearing how bad my company was, how bad I am, and how I'd done so many things wrong. I'd lost clients and employees, all people I very much care about. I couldn't wrap my head around what was going on. Even after we'd brought about our clients' success, I was told to my face that we hadn't, which simply didn't make any sense.

By Halloween, between the harassment emails, hateful words, and two abrupt cancellations for absolutely no reason, I was at a total loss. I went trick-or-treating that night with my son, then retreated while the boys stayed out. I sat with GG at the house, passing out candy, and between kids coming to the door, I opened up to her.

"I feel like I've gotten this all wrong. I've messed everything up. I feel like I've wasted the last five years of my life. All the sacrifice, everything that I did to grow and scale this company, all just to be sitting here, shedding clients and employees, being told hateful, hurtful things. We gave up trying to have a second child—should we have worked harder to have a second or even third?

"I don't know what God has in store for me. On one hand, I'm having such a great time working for Payroll Network. They're such a joy to work with, and everything's going extremely well. On the other hand, in my own company, I'm being told hateful, hurtful things, and clients are ripping up contracts that don't even have a termination clause. I'm not strong enough to deal with this. I'm just not built for it. Some business owners may be, but not me. This is crushing me." Over and over, I asked GG, in a variety of ways, "Have I made a terrible mistake?" I spent all of Halloween questioning the entire trajectory of the last five years of my life, and GG helped me by creating a space where I could talk it all out.

In the first week of November, I was still in a deep state of reflection, questioning what to do with the next stage of my life. I was just a week and a half away from my thirty-ninth birthday, and my company was about to turn five years old. I started to feel like a new season was coming. I reached out to a couple of friends, simply seeking perspective and wise counsel.

I didn't like making a lot of money from clients who were ultimately unhappy with what I'd sold them.

When I talked to Doug again, I told him, "I need help. I'm at a low. My clients seem to hate me, and at the very least, they're accusing me of things that aren't true. If they're using this all as a tactic to get out of their contracts, that's one thing. But gosh, if they're *really* being sincere and this is *their* truth, that's even worse. I feel like a failure more than anything for building a company that everyone apparently hates."

I had to take stock. I'd had a high-performing sales career, and I'd left it because I was frustrated that I was selling a product that operations couldn't support. I didn't like making a lot of money from clients who were ultimately unhappy with what I'd sold them. The main reason I started my own company was to sit in the business development seat, do sales, and be in charge of delivering quality service. I have such high standards, and the whole idea was for those very standards to ensure that we maintained a thoroughly excellent product.

Now, in a way, I'd found myself right where I had been five years prior, and *that* was when I realized, *Maybe entrepreneurship isn't for me anymore. Maybe I gave it my best go. Maybe God's closing the door on this.* I still had Payroll Network, who loved me and had expressed interest in having me work for them full time. I was still in a state of deep reflection when talking this all over with David, my friends, and my coach.

I couldn't help but consider that maybe God had something different in store for me. More and more, I wanted to transition into a quieter chapter, without the stress and strain, where God could work through me and where I wouldn't be as distracted. My head had been down in the weeds for so long that I hadn't had the time to hear from him. Instead of sitting in his Word, it had just been go, go, go, seven days a week.

On the way home from a business trip with one of our fractional CROs, Kristin, I began to open up about wanting to be a CRO and not a CEO. I asked her for her opinion about having the employees buy my equity and becoming owners. She thought that idea had potential, so in order to get a fair market valuation, I reached back out to my business broker and said I wanted to list the company again.

By doing this, I would put my fate into God's hands, but I also wanted to be responsible and follow whatever outcome God wanted for me. I listed the company at a far smaller price than before. My hope was to receive a full-price letter of intent (LOI) at $1.5 million and use that as a baseline for the valuation of my company. From there, I could build a new structure where employees could buy in, and if they didn't have the means or desire to fully buy me out, I could look for an equity partner.

None of this would have been possible if I had not reached a new level of clarity in October, when things started to turn around. We began hiring tremendous new talent and wound up with three former CEOs who had already scaled and exited other companies while sitting in CRO seats. We brought on unbelievable CMO-level marketing talent—all scrappy, entrepreneurial, and willing to work. We onboarded two new clients, which helped offset the expenses of our new hires. Many of our clients continued to struggle due to the state of the economy. Most businesses, especially small businesses, were missing their revenue targets, struggling to bring on new clients, or losing their existing clients left and right. Of course, we understood, because we'd been through it ourselves.

I received an offer at my new price of $1.5 million, but the man who wanted to buy my company reminded me of Hulk Hogan and was very condescending: "Hey there, little lady." He noted how "brave" I was in our first meeting and said I was making the right decision to sell because it's so hard for a woman to be a CEO. "It's a big role—you should probably just go on and do something else."

Unfortunately, he was right: it *is* a big role, and I *didn't* want to do it anymore. But the way he said it—I couldn't handle it. I told my broker to just hold on to his offer as leverage but had no intention whatsoever of selling to him.

That experience made me increasingly interested in selling the company to my employees. Then, a woman named Jennifer reached out to me with a connection to a local investor who'd sold his own professional services company—one a lot like ours, but in IT. He was working as an investor and an advisor and had been looking into buying a marketing company.

When we hopped on a call, I fell in love with the potential of his offer. It felt so right—all my employees could stay in their current spots and retain their authority, without a new owner coming in and telling everybody what to do. The investor just wanted to be a silent partner while acting as an advisor and injecting cash into the company. The deal would allow me to go work full time for Payroll Network and to install a CEO in my absence. Everything sounded so good. I prayed on it. I laid everything at God's feet and said, *Whatever you want, let's make it happen.*

Then, as negotiations continued, it became clear that if I moved forward with that deal, I'd be left with virtually nothing after taxes and fees, so I ruled it out. The next option was to hold on to it, sell a *portion* to the employees, resign as CEO, and install my replacement. I could sell majority equity to an investor in the future, but I could resign as CEO now, stay on as a founder, and install a replacement CEO. In the meantime, everything felt right with Payroll Network. At the end of December, I accepted their full-time offer for a January 30 start date.

CHAPTER

23

CHAPTER 23

I didn't make this decision lightly. In fact, I was in such disarray in making the decision to resign as the House of Revenue CEO and go work at Payroll Network that I was making myself sick. I was praying and praying and praying, asking the Lord for direction, even though being a CEO exhausted me and whittled me down to nothing. I committed to the Lord in my prayer: *If this is where you want me to be, I will continue to serve you in this seat. If this is not where you want me to be, then please open the next door and make the path clear for me.*

The problem was that *both* doors were wide open. House of Revenue turned around to the extent that it felt like an entirely new company all over again. I could stay, but I simply didn't see myself in the leader's seat anymore. The people at Payroll Network are beautiful, lovely, wonderful people and welcomed me with open arms. I knew I could bring so much value to their operation and knew that I could help them succeed.

I often found myself down on my knees, praying. *God, just please tell me what to do.* My girlfriend, Ana, has played such an important role as a spiritual leader in my life, and during this time, we went and had what turned into a three-hour lunch in which I laid out my heart to her regarding how much I was struggling with the decision.

She told me, "Let me pray for you over the next couple of weeks, and we'll see if the Lord reveals anything to me. If He does, I'll let you know." Then, she sent me a video that I've listened to multiple times since. Every word in the video was so relevant to my life. It spoke about how God was moving in my life, helping me move into a season of financial security and stability. As I was listening, I was thinking, *This is so me. I feel so led to do this.* At the end of the day, I'll do anything the Lord wants me to do. I'm here to serve him.

I can take on a lot, especially when it comes to risk. But doing so as a CEO nearly killed me.

I've proved myself over and over again. I tend to be successful at everything that I do, and I say that humbly. God has gifted me unbelievable talents and a competitive spirit that loves to win. I've proved, at least by the world's standards, that I can be successful against all odds. I don't know many people who could have done what I've done. I can take on a lot, especially when it comes to risk. But doing so as a CEO nearly killed me. I've been in the pit of despair, on my knees, asking God to take control of my life, unsure of whether I could stand to live another day.

I had hated my company and my job. I would've quit a hundred times if I hadn't been the owner. There were days when I was so numb and depressed—I was there physically, but not mentally or emotionally. But God does not waste any stress or strife in our lives. He uses it for good. Knowing that helped me endure. So I prayed to the Lord, and I asked Ana to pray for me. *Please. Whatever I'm supposed to do, show me the way.*

I wanted the Lord to know I loved him above all else and that I just wanted to be where he wanted me to be, because I knew that was where I would unlock never-ending abundance and joy. At this point, that's the only thing I want in my life. Trust me: nothing compares. Not the new house I'm building, not the car that I drive, not even my amazing husband or my loving, caring son. The Lord is above all else for me.

Ana texted me in the middle of December and said, *I want to hop on a call with you if you have time.* Of course I had time—I knew she was ready to talk to me about what had been revealed to her. She's a very, very spiritual woman, and I trust her completely.

"I feel like the Lord's revealed to me something very special for you," she said.

Like what?

"He's giving you the opportunity to choose, which is not something he does for a lot of people. It is a sign that he trusts you and that you've been obedient, and that he knows your heart. I believe that he's *letting* you choose."

I broke down, sighed the biggest sigh of relief, and cried out of both joy and gratefulness. Finally, I knew that this whole struggle wasn't about what I was going to do for a living—it was about who I was going to be when I walked through the door. I knew in that moment that God trusts me, whether I work at Starbucks, become a stay-at-home mom, or work in ministry. Whether I'm a CEO, CRO, salesperson, teacher, or volunteer, it ultimately doesn't matter. I finally felt peace in my heart that God loves and trusts me, knows how much I love him, that I'm living my life in partnership with him, and that my number one goal in the world is to spread the good news of the gospel.

I will not be the Christian that pushes people away. I will be the kind of Christian that will walk like Jesus, talk like Jesus, and love everybody, no matter what. It is my number one responsibility to point people to the gospel of the Word of God and show them the true love of Jesus—and that's it.

He saved my life, and now here I sit with the greatest peace I've ever had, looking at a job offer that's so generous, stepping down from a company I've built that's in the absolute best place it could ever possibly be. I hold my head high. I finished my job. Now it's a new season, with a new team, a new community, all of whom can experience the love and light of Jesus through our interactions and my leadership.

I will falter. I will make mistakes. I will be envious. I will even judge. I will probably use a tone of voice that I won't be proud of later. I'll make mistakes—after all, I'm human. The only perfect one is God himself. I can only hope that my style of grace and leadership will allow others to bestow grace and mercy upon *me* when I falter.

This will be the greatest assignment I've ever taken on. It's a huge role with a big title, but I'm ready to step into it, and I'm ready to lead. I'm ready to do remarkable work. I'm ready to lead at a level that will make people say, "There's something different about her." And when they spend enough time with me, they'll realize it has nothing to do with me and everything to do with the love and light of the Lord Jesus Christ in my heart—and that same love and light is an open invitation to all.

All this is a full confirmation that everything I have comes from the Lord. And with this, I decided to give the company to the employees instead of sell any portion of my equity or take on an investor. I don't need to fight to make money or get a big payout. I already *have* the payout. I've already won the lottery. I've already won the game. I will never be without. It is not worth harming relationships with my employees or my clients to sell the company. It is only right that it continues to live on with the people who stood by my side over the last six months and fought the battle with me to keep this intact.

For years, I was for myself. Why? Isn't that what we are supposed to do? Fight to get ahead? Do everything we can to succeed? Win at all costs? Make something of ourselves? Put self-care first? Be responsible for our own self-esteem and self-worth? I found, over and over again, that that's exhausting and not even close to what life is about. I'm sorry if that's a buzzkill, but as it turns out, it's not about me—and it's not about you either.

If we continue to strive to achieve goals for ourselves, chasing our personal agendas for our own personal gains, we will be left hungry, thirsty, empty, and confused as to why everything we accomplish never satisfies our souls or our innermost beings. What a sad life we will have lived if, at the end, all we have to show for it is money, fame, and recognition. At the end of that kind of life, we'll have to acknowledge that we've failed ourselves, our families, and the people around us. Is money bad? No. But of course, the *love* of money is the root of all evil. It breeds greed, competition, selfishness, hate, comparison, jealousy, gossip, and defeat, among so many other things.

It's crazy to believe that as a self-proclaimed Christian, I still falter. I make mistakes. I battle the flesh versus spirit every day. I pray and beg God to purify my heart and remove the temptation and desire of money, fame, and recognition. I pray that the Lord will guide me, reveal his vision for me, build the path under my feet, and prevent me from taking the wheel, attempting to steer the ship of my life, run it off the rails, and crash and burn—all over again.

Yet it still happens. Have I not learned? God's grace is sufficient. *All I need is him.* Yet I go through seasons—some where I'm obedient, full of his grace, confident in my voice, and filled with passion for the Lord and his goodness. I rise above stressful situations, and they don't faze me. I believe my provision comes from the Lord and that he will take care of my every need.

Then, without fail, the stress and strain of being a wife, mom, and professional begins to chip away at me, and I become weak. I start to believe the weight of the business, my family, and everyone's well-being is my responsibility. Where do these lies come from? The enemy, of course—the enemy hates my love for God's goodness and my love for him. The enemy knows the well-worn paths to get me to believe in lies, and manages to convince me, all over again, that I'm not good enough and that nothing I can do will ever get me to the top.

Then, what do I do next? I put myself in the driver's seat, start making frantic, reactive decisions in an all-too-human attempt to "fix" everything, which does exactly the opposite of what I'm trying to accomplish. Why am I telling you this? Because I'd be a fool to paint a picture, as an openly faith-based CEO, that I have it all together and figured out or that my life is perfect.

What I will tell you is that *my life has been worth it.* It's worth it to be obedient and praise and worship the Lord through both the highs and the lows. I will also tell you that the Bible is the perfect guidebook to a beautiful life that's worth living. I myself am living proof that when one abides by and follows God's Word, life is stress-free and free of worry. Things still go wrong, but we can respond knowing that everything is in God's hands no matter what.

As I come off the heels of yet another season of panic, worry, guilt, shame, and a pervasive fear of losing it all, the irony is that I already *have* it all. All I need is him. I am for him. I am for his people.

CHAPTER 23

I am for love, compassion, serving, and being his love and light. God is so good. When I fully surrender to Him, my life becomes so pure and beautiful that I can't help but sit in utter awe and cry from the overwhelming joy that pours out of me.

I want my life to be an example of a woman who fights the good fight and makes mistakes, yet manages to love fearlessly and has been chosen in her way by God to model for you what that fight looks like. I am here to give you encouragement that he is worth it and that the fight is worth it. Praise Jesus for my hardships. They have allowed me to be his voice for anyone who reads this.

I feel like the Lord is having me step into a new season, one where I can simplify my life. I had a heart-to-heart with my husband, and we decided that we're going to take our time to figure out what the Lord has in store for him next and what he's going to do for a living.

> **I feel like the Lord is having me step into a new season, one where I can simplify my life.**

I'm hanging up my CEO hat—proudly. Holding my head high, I'll retain my founder title and get to be a part of this beautiful company that we rebuilt, as an advisor. Occasionally, I'll work out of the House of Revenue office, because Payroll Network is located in Maryland and I can't work from home every day or I will lose my sanity.

Giving the company to the employees and walking away from a potential million-plus-dollar payout gives me the peace to know my actions prove the team means more to me than money ever will. I love those people and am grateful for their contributions.

As I look forward, I'm looking at getting more invested in my son's life. After averaging eighty hours a week this year, I'm transitioning to a forty-hour per week job as a CRO, which for me feels like

273

a half-time job. Going from being a CEO and entrepreneur, risking it all every day, is tough, and I'm ready to sit in a quieter seat and simplify my life.

We're finishing up the remodel on the house on the hill that we bought. We'll move in, then finally sell our current house. It's a season for me to simplify, make time, be with the Lord, my husband, my son, and our family. I invested nearly all my time and energy into scaling my company. Today it's profitable and healthy, and our employees *and* clients are happy. The work they're doing now is so good. All over again, everyone's happy—my people are happy, our clients are happy, and *I'm* happy.

The Lord has opened the door for me to do work that will be fulfilling, where I can provide a tremendous amount of value. He has taken care of me, and now, in turn, I will take care of my family and my new team. My life and my decisions should be proof that there's a very different way to live.

CHAPTER

24

CHAPTER 24

There's a long tattoo on my left arm that says, "Be who you could have become," and the story behind it is one worth telling.

Christina Hall is the name of a celebrity I follow from HGTV. She used to be married to Tarek El Moussa, and they had that show called *Flip or Flop*. She's currently on husband number three and has dealt with a lot of public scrutiny toward her and her marriages, and I love how gracefully she's handled it.

In spring of 2021, somewhere around her thirty-eighth birthday, partly to combat the stress and anxiety that had built up in her life after publicly going through *two* divorces, she revealed that she'd smoked venom from a bufo toad. A lot of celebrities, from Mike Tyson to Tony Robbins, have done the same. Doing so is supposed to make you feel as though you've died, are no longer living inside of your body or your earthly self. Your spirit ascends and is transformed into pure light.

You're one with nature and the creator, and it's apparently such a healing and euphoric experience that it wipes your slate clean. All the crud that accumulates in people's lives—all the oppression, fear, anxiety, depression—goes momentarily flying out the window. People see that the weight of worrying about our challenges and what people think of us are fundamentally products of our own minds.

Obviously, after reading about how healing this toad-venom experience was for Christina Hall, I was intrigued. I went straight to listening to Mike Tyson talking to Tony Robbins about doing it, and more and more I found myself thinking, *Gosh, I really want to do this.*

The weight of worrying about our challenges and what people think of us are fundamentally products of our own minds.

The only problem is that it's illegal. I believe it's been decriminalized in California, but in most of the United States, it's fully illegal. I started praying and asking God to give me that kind of experience, without having to figure out how to go to California to do something that was otherwise illegal. God is the creator and all powerful, and I knew he could do it if he felt like it would help me. I prayed and prayed and prayed, and then, around a week later, I had a dream.

In the dream, as Beckham, David, and I were standing in a room, a cartoon character entered into the scene with a cartoon bazooka, which he shot at all three of us. At that point, we changed from lifelike humans into Tom-and-Jerry-style cartoons. All three of us were riddled with bullet holes from the cartoon bazooka, which disintegrated what I'll call our outer shields. The human sides of us fell to the ground, just like in a cartoon, to reveal our inner souls as beams of pure light.

I disconnected from David and Beckham, and my spirit ascended as a bright light to become one with nature. I *became* part of a beautiful scene: there was a forest, tall grasses, the sun peeking through a canopy of trees, and a river running right through all of it.

It felt as though my purest self was present right there with God the Creator himself, calm as can be. We proceeded to have a casual conversation about life, what was troubling me, and all the weight and guilt that I'd been feeling. Then he said something to me that I'll never forget. He told me that I'd meet him again in a very similar spot when I'm done with my time on earth, and that when I see him again, my biggest regret will be realizing how easy it would have been to honor and serve him, spreading the good news of the gospel, and saving people's souls.

He reminded me that I'm his servant, and that he acknowledges my good works. He said that he loved my obedience but felt like I was limiting myself by carrying around so much weight, trying to please people, wanting to conform to the world. My focus on being a CEO, being a high performer, obsessing over revenue, growth, profitability, and all the stress and strain therein had become my guiding light, *instead* of him.

He said that the biggest regret I'd have in the end would be putting so much care into worldly things, all as a result of fearing man instead of fearing the Lord himself. In my experience on earth, I would continue to be tempted and weighed down by what the world wants from me, or thinks of me, and in the end, I would come to regret all of it.

"I will see you again," he told me, "and it will be right here. I will reveal to you how easy it would have been to drop the weight of the world and graciously serve me all your days—without any titles, without the need to feel certain, or to chase status, money, recognition, or be anything beyond who you already are."

Who I was with Him in that moment is all I ever needed. When I woke up, it all felt so fresh and so real. It sparked a realization that I needed to start living my life differently. Yet at the time, it was spring of 2021, and I was still trapped inside of what my business had become. Growth was killing us, and I was trapped. My twenty-eight employees and their families depended on me. Even after having this vision in which the Lord spoke so clearly to me, I remained a slave to the business and what I'd created. Soon after, I suffered that famous mental breakdown at Disneyland.

Around three months later, in January 2022, I attended a workshop that my Titan CEO group put together. The keynote speaker came up to do a slideshow, and his first slide said, "At the end of your life, if you get to meet the person you could've become, are you going to be looking in the mirror or will you see someone completely different?" Those words just pierced me—many months after having that dream, God was again trying to get my attention. I realized from that moment that we were about to go down a new path, one upon which he was going to help me create a new life.

One month later, a tattoo artist came into town from LA. His work is unbelievable, and I decided to get on his schedule. He created a tattoo for me: *Be who you could have become.* It's a constant reminder: to not fear man, to not run a business that the world expects, that the Lord himself is all I need, and that he is going to guide and create with me—through him and with him.

It reminds me that together, the Lord and I will do extraordinary things in all facets of life, as long as I remain fully surrendered to him. Even though I'm still a broken sinner, make mistakes, fall, and falter, my tattoo is a constant reminder to serve him and to live for him and that he will do good works through me as long as I remain available to him.

In the end, when I see him again, I want to be able to tell him that I'm so glad I woke up, made the decision to truly be a disciple, follow him, carry out his good works, and spread the good news of the gospel to the ends of the earth. My hope is that I'll ultimately be able to look back and say, "You were right. It **was** easy."

AFTERWORD

I've learned that life has a funny way of working out. God's plans are always better than mine. As you read in the book, with all the best of intentions, I hoped to gift the company to the employees. But within weeks of finishing the book, our company was affected by economic and market uncertainty, causing us to take a significant revenue loss in the first quarter of the year and resort to considering all options. To learn how it all played out, connect with me at marygrothe.com and read my blog.